Cultural Constructions of 'Woman'

Cultural Constructions of 'Woman'

Pauline Kolenda
University of Houston

Sheffield Publishing Company
Salem, Wisconsin

For information about this book, write or call:
Sheffield Publishing Company
P.O. Box 359
Salem, Wisconsin 53168

(414) 843-2281

Cover by Janice van Mechelen.

ISBN 0-88133-306-9

Printed in the United States of America.

CULTURAL CONSTRUCTIONS OF 'WOMAN'

Pauline Kolenda, Editor

CONTENTS

The other authors of this volume dedicate it to the memory of two of the authors, Helge Pross and Joan M. McCrea, both of whom died in 1984.

The papers in this volume were first presented at a conference on the anthropology of women at the University of Houston - University Park in February 1981. Since that time two of the authors, Helge Pross and Joan M. McCrea, have died, both victims of cancer. We dedicate this book to their memories. The papers by Davis-Floyd, Edwards, and Qvarfort and Kolenda have been brought up to a mid-1980s date for this publication.

We owe thanks to Professor George Daly, then Dean of the College of Social Sciences, who provided the budget for the Houston conference, to Nancy Edwards who voluntarily helped with much of the organization of the conference, as well as to Harriet Aldstadt and Pat McQuillan in the Office of Social Sciences, many students of anthropology including Carol Bahm, Angela Leggett, Kathy Reese, Nancy Sharp, Babette Streiker, Debra Ward, Robert Ward, Beatrice Weaver, Sarah Sewing and Terry Alford, my colleagues in the Anthropology Department at the University of Houston, Elliece Hopkins, Russell Reid, Robert Randall, Kenneth Brown, Norris Lang, and Anthony Colson, all of whom helped in many ways.

Permission for the publication of Judith K. Brown's "Cross-Cultural Perspectives on Middle-Aged Women" was granted by the University of Chicago Press. Permission to include the table from Bacdayan's treatment of the Bontoc was granted by Columbia University Press.

The problems are the same in various countries, but the attempts at solution are diverse and slow. They can be speeded up by the adaptation of successful and productive experiments from one country to another. Therefore, a wide exchange of information and research findings can stimulate progress in every country.

Joan M. McCrea (1977: Swedish Labor Market Policy for Women," *Labor and Society* 2: 377)

Introduction

Pauline Kolenda, Editor

The anthropology of women, as a special sub-field of anthropology, began with the publication of two important collections of papers and one far-ranging cross-cultural investigation. Although there were other important books, Michelle Rosaldo and Louise Lamphere's *Women, Culture and Society* (1974), Rayna Reiter's *Toward an Anthropology of Women* (1975), and Kay Martin and Barbara Voorhies' *Female of the Species* (1975) set a number of the issues which preoccupied subsequent writers. One has been the issue of the contribution made by each sex to human evolution, resulting first from their respective roles in the major human adaptation, foraging for food, as well as, second, from the likely "natures" of the two sexes in the eras of earliest humanity.

The first began as a response to the conference volume, *Man the Hunter* (1968). Lee and DeVore, in their editors' introduction, pointed out that for over 90 percent of the human career, people had lived by hunting and gathering. Only for the past 12,000 years, out of their more than two million years, had people had horticulture, agriculture, herding and machine-powered industry. Washburn and Lancaster specified some of the skills which men developed by hunting, important since humans were evolving as a species physically and mentally during the eons when hunting was men's main occupation. Sally Slocum in "Woman the Gatherer" (in the Reiter volume) responded to the implication of their assertions--that women's work had *not* been important in human evolution. Many writers have added to her claim that it was females' caring for their offspring who had probably been the core of earliest society, that gathering required much knowledge of plants and insects, as well as considerable eye-hand coordination, that the net bag as an earliest "tool" was probably a female invention, as eventually was the growing of plants. If one accepted the concept that the activities of the species contributed to its physical, including mental, evolution, then early female human activities could be understood as making important contributions just as plausibly as could male humans' hunting activity.

Related to the sex and evolution question also has been the issue of the "nature," presumably given genetically, of the two sexes. What was each sex like before culture began? Studies of the non-human primates, especially of chimpanzees and baboons, have been undertaken and searched for evidence suggesting the sexual nature of earliest humanity, on the assumption that chimpanzees and baboons are contemporary primates with little culture, and hence perhaps are similar to early human kind before our species had much in the way of culture (invented and then learned and transmitted ways of doing things). Enough such studies have been done by now that there are many unresolved contradictions (e.g., McGrew 1981, Zihlman 1981) among the findings, and hardly a clear message about the sexual natures of early human men and women.

Other concerns within the anthropology of women have included the egalitarian relations between the sexes in a category of cultures with a common economic-ecological base, namely the foraging societies; the higher status of women in matrilineal societies; and the relativity of women's economic and political power to the technical-economic-ecological adaptation of a culture. The latter was thoroughly explored in Martin and Voorhies' book, but has also been elaborated importantly in Peggy Sanday's *Female Power and Male Dominance* (1981).

Sanday goes beyond an ecological approach in her combining it with a symbolic one. Her book thus reflects another theme in the anthropology of women, that of symbols of women. Earlier works such as Mervyn Meggitt's (1964) study of sexual relations among the Mae Enga of highland New Guinea with its emphasis on female pollution, as well as Mary Douglas' *Purity and Danger* (1966), stimulated responses like Faithorn's on the Kăfe of New Guinea; she explicated the complexity of beliefs about pollution among the Kăfe, showing that both sexes had the capacity to pollute each other and to pollute aspects of nature (Faithorn in the Reiter volume). The symbolic anthropologist, Claude Lévi-Strauss inspired Gayle Rubin's "Traffic in Women" (in the Reiter volume), her protest against male control of marital arrangements; and his nature versus culture binary opposition inspired

Sherry Ortner's "Is Female to Male as Nature is to Culture?" (in the Rosaldo-Lamphere volume), which, in turn, stimulated several objections including a volume of papers, MacCormack and Strathern's *Nature, Culture and Gender* (1980). Women are a popular topic for symbolic anthropological treatments, and discourse about symbols and women is well-advanced.

One of the most impressive features of the anthropology of women has been the rediscovery of vast amounts of ethnography that speak to the question: are there cultures, or have there been cultures, in which women have had equal status with men? From the volumes by Sanday (1981), Leacock (1981), and Dahlberg (1981), one must add to the famous Iroquois (Brown in Reiter), several other Native American groups in which women had substantial public power--the Wyandot of the Huron, the Montagnais-Naskapi of Labrador, the Cherokee and Arapaho, as well as African kingdoms like the Ashanti, Dahomey, and Igbo that had institutionalized positions for women leaders in dual-sex governments. There are now known to have been several cultures in which women were regularly hunters (Estioko-Griffin and Griffin in Dahlberg) or warriors (Sanday).

A conclusion that has now been repudiated was a premature conclusion that women were universally subordinated to men (Rosaldo and Lamphere). A number of women anthropologists have disagreed, including Sanday, Leacock, and especially Schlegel (1977) in her collection, *Sexual Stratification.*

These issues within the anthropology of women have been largely intra-field relevant--they speak to concerns of anthropologists on classic topics and works within anthropology. They, of course, have extra-field relevance for people in general, but their import is to affect the general understanding of human sexes across time and across cultures. They are background to action.

The papers in the present volume are meant to be relevant to action, action relating to the daily lives of women in America in the 1980s and 1990s. As a whole, the volume takes a new approach, although the influence of the forerunners, briefly summarized above, inheres in the papers. We are asking: What can American women learn from women in the rest of the world? In what way can ethnographic data and anthropological approaches enlighten us about the situation of ordinary American women? How can anthropology relate to the problems of contemporary American women and to some of the women's issues of our times?

The essays in *Cultural Constructions of 'Woman'* are directly or indirectly critical of American society as it treats women. There is a long tradition in anthropology of relating its knowledge to our own society. One of the most illustrious practitioners was the late Margaret Mead. Anthropologists may either make studies of peoples within American society, or they may have insights into our culture, because of their capacity to see their own culture more clearly because of a kind of detachment and perspective that develops in the course of studying strange, unfamiliar cultures. Clyde Kluckhohn thirty years ago entitled his introduction to anthropology, *A Mirror for Man,* meaning that we could understand ourselves by learning about other versions of the human species. In this volume, anthropological reflexivity takes various forms.

Robbie Davis-Floyd is inspired by Brigitte Jordan's *Birth in Four Cultures.* In that, a work both of medical anthropology and the anthropology of women, Jordan contrasts American birthing with the way it is done among the Maya of Yucatan, and among the Dutch and the Swedes; their ways are in many ways more humane than ours, more caring about new mothers. Davis-Floyd goes beyond Jordan in doing field work with pregnant women while she herself was pregnant. She interviewed fifty women in three different American cities, as they went through pregnancy, childbirth and early child-care. She does not stop, however, with her fifty informants but follows the issues they raised and those she herself perceived in the course of her study, going into the medical literature on childbirth, consulting physicians, to contrast the "official" medical view with the consensus of her informants.

In the second paper, Judith K. Brown, like Martin and Voorhies, Peggy Sanday, and her own earlier work, takes a cross-cultural comparative approach, in this case toward the issue of the status of older women. In the United States, it is the past-forties women who have been largely ignored either in the general public discussion about women or in the women's movement. The weight of Brown's evidence raises the question: If women in other societies have responsibility and influence in middle and old age, why not here?

In the third paper, we find Kathlyn Zahniser doing what Alan Holmberg called participant-intervention in the sense that she was not only a participant-observer but was herself the experimental stimulus under study, as she entered occupations that had become established as male preserves. Her experience reflects the fact that there is no unanimity among American males in their responses to such innovations. Within our own culture, women may be treated well or badly depending upon the ideology of the actors involved. The weight of her ordeal is to reveal the truth that it is not the difficulty of the skills of the job that are daunting for women in blue-collar occupations, but the barrier of the male co-workers' informal subculture, as well as the prejudices of the male boss.

The last three papers are concerned with the equality of women in public life in three different societies. Both the Philippines and Sweden are countries in which, it has been claimed, there is equality for women with men. Edwards, who did ethnographic and linguistic field work in the Zamboanga area of Mindanao in the Philippines, and Qvarfort and McCrea, both of whom are economists specializing on Swedish women in the labor force, examine such claims for these two often-idealized regions. We may ask why Filipino groups resisted the subordination of women that the adoption of Christianity and Islam might well have entailed. The fact that these great world religions do subordinate women is especially clear when we see cultures which are Christian and Islamic but which have not adopted the usual subordination of women, as in the Philippines. The Philippines is part of a larger geographical area in which equality of the sexes has been widespread--Southeast Asia and the Pacific.

We may identify rather readily with Sweden as a European culture similar to our own. The way in which Sweden outstrips the United States in government-insured rights and concern for women raises the question of whether America will follow. West Germany is more like America than is Sweden in the situation for women. Helge Pross, a German sociologist, tells us that German women are eager to join the world outside the home but that surveys show that German men still idealize the homemaker. Will the attitudes of the two sexes continue to diverge as women become more eager for release from the home while men obdurately want her there?

The papers in this book are especially related to American women's situation in the 1980s and 1990s--the issue of birthing when women more than ever want the birth experience to be emotionally fulfilling, the issue of middle age as women in the United States live longer and are returning for more education and getting more education than ever before, the issue of women in occupations traditionally male, the issue of government guarantees of rights for women.

The French anthropologist, Claude Lévi-Strauss, in his book *The Savage Mind* says, ". . . terms never have intrinsic meaning; their meaning is 'positional,' a function of history and cultural context on the one hand, and on the other of the structure of the system in which they are called upon to appear" (1962: 74). This orientation seems useful in considering the concept of woman, as a 'term' that has little 'intrinsic meaning.' Lévi-Strauss himself pondered the diversity and seeming arbitrariness of various cultures' constructions of the gender roles for females and males. Margaret Mead very early also devoted herself to this issue. She wrote, for example:

> With the paucity of material for elaboration, no culture has failed to seize upon the conspicuous facts of age and sex in some way, whether it be the convention of one Philippine tribe that no man can keep a secret, the Manus assumption that only men enjoy playing with babies, the Toda prescription of almost all domestic work as too sacred for women, or the Arapesh insistence that women's heads are stronger than men's. (Mead 1963: xi)

It is my hope that the juxtaposition of the constructions of woman in Western cultures with those in non-Western cultures may make the lesson take, that the category of woman, like other terms with little intrinsic meaning, is a cultural construct, created and recreated throughout a culture's history, and related to the other aspects of the totality of a culture.

References Cited

Brown, Judith K.
1963 A Cross-cultural Study of Female Initiation Rites. American Anthropologist 65: 837-862.

1975 Iroquois Women: An Ethnohistoric Note. *In* Reiter (below).

Dahlberg, Frances, editor
1981 Woman the Gatherer. New Haven: Yale University Press.

Douglas, Mary
1966 Purity and Danger. London: Routledge and Kegan Paul.

Estioko-Griffin, Agnes and P. Bion Griffin
1981 Woman the Hunter: The Agta. *In* Dahlberg.

Faithorn, Elizabeth
1975 The Concept of Pollution among the Kafe of the Papua New Guinea Highlands. *In* Reiter (below).

Holmberg, Alan
1955 Participant Intervention in the Field. Human Organization 14:23-26.

Kluckhohn, Clyde
1949 Mirror for Man. New York: Whittlesey House.

Leacock, Eleanor Burke
1981 Myths of Male Dominance: Collected Articles on Women Cross Culturally. New York: Monthly Review Press.

Lee, Richard and Irven DeVore
1969 Man the Hunter. Chicago: Aldine.

Levi-Strauss, Claude
1962 The Savage Mind. Chicago: University of Chicago Press.

1969 The Elementary Structures of Kinship. Boston: Beacon Press.

Martin, Kay and Barbara Voorhies
1975 Female of the Species. New York: Columbia University Press.

MacCormack, Carol and Marilyn Strathern
1980 Nature, Culture and Gender. Cambridge: Cambridge University Press.

McGrew, W. C.
1981 The Female Chimpanzee as a Human Evolutionary Prototype. *In* Dahlberg (above).

Mead, Margaret
1963 Sex and Temperament in Three Primitive Societies. New York: William Morrow.

Meggitt, M. J.
1964 Male-Female Relationships in the Highlands of Australian New Guinea. American Anthropologist 66 (4), part 2: 204-224.

Ortner, Sherry B.
1974 Is Female to Male as Nature is to Culture? *In* Rosaldo and Lamphere (below).

Reiter, Rayna, editor
1975 Toward an Anthropology of Women. New York: Monthly Review Press.

Rosaldo, Michelle and Louise Lamphere, editors
1974 Woman, Culture and Society. Stanford: Stanford University Press.

Sanday, Peggy Reeves
1981 Female Power and Male Dominance. Cambridge: Cambridge University Press.

Slocum, Sally
1975 Woman the Gatherer: Male Bias in Anthropology. *In* Reiter (above).

Washburn, Sherwood and C. Lancaster
1968 The Evolution of Hunting. *In* Lee and DeVore (above).

Zihlman, Adrienne L.
1981 Women as Shapers of the Human Adaptation. *In* Dahlberg (above).

Pregnancy and Cultural Confusion: Contradictions in Socialization

Robbie Davis-Floyd

> . . . if we consider the sparse ethnographic record, we find that there is no known society where birth is treated, by the people involved in its doing, as a merely physiological function. On the contrary, it is everywhere socially marked and shaped (Jordan 1980: 1)

In modern American society, pregnancy is a natural condition treated unnaturally, a physiological process imbued with magic and taboo, an experience belonging uniquely to women, yet all too often removed from their control. Using data from women of three cities, I will discuss the process by which educated, middle-class American women are socialized into pregnancy and childbirth. This process is a focal point for cultural paradox. Pregnancy, like any life-crisis rite of passage, places the woman in a special transitional realm as she moves from one state to another. In this realm, she--and her partner--become peculiarly vulnerable to the conflicts inherent in the American cultural perceptions of pregnancy and birth.

Specifically, I shall try to demonstrate first that pregnancy, birth, and the newborn phase of motherhood together constitute a single life-crisis rite of passage involving major changes of state and status *for the woman;* yet, today, in American society, this rite of passage is culturally perceived as properly belonging under the tutelage and control of the medical profession. Its stages are marked in medical terms in a gradually intensifying process that climaxes in a near-complete medical takeover of the most significant and intensely transformative phase of the entire rite of passage--the birth experience. Thereby the woman is frequently denied the powerful internal experience of growth and change that worldwide seems to be the most important function of this initiatory type of *rite de passage* (Turner 1972; Eliade 1975). Turner has written:

> This term "to grow" well expresses how many peoples think of transition rites. We are inclined, as sociologists, to reify our abstractions (it is indeed a device which helps us to understand many kinds of social interconnection) and to talk about persons "moving through structural positions in a hierarchical frame" and the like. Not so the Bemba and the Shilluk of the Sudan who see the status or condition embodied or incarnate, if you like, *in* the person. To "grow" a girl into a woman is to effect an ontological transformation; it is not merely to convey an unchanging substance from one position to another by a quasi-mechanical force. . . . It is the ritual and the esoteric teaching which grows girls and makes men. It is ritual, too, which among Shilluk makes a prince into a king, or, among Luvale, a cultivator into a hunter. The arcane knowledge of "gnosis" obtained in the liminal period is felt to change the inmost nature of the neophyte, impressing him, as a seal impresses wax, with the characteristics of his new state. It is not a mere acquisition of knowledge, but a change in being (Turner 1964: 11).

I shall demonstrate secondly that there are four separate but overlapping and often contradictory socialization processes for the pregnant woman involving four major interactional domains: 1) the public; 2) the medical--doctor's offices and hospitals; 3) the formally educative--books, prepared childbirth classes; and 4) what I will call the collective or the folk--informal relationships with other women who are either pregnant or have young children. These four socialization processes relate to four conflicting and contradictory cultural views of pregnancy as: 1) a social/ritual process in which intensely personal transformations must become symbolic public transformations; 2) a medical event, a pathological process requiring constant supervision and often intervention by members of the medical profession; 3) a "natural" process that is best left entirely alone to proceed according to nature's decrees, but that can nevertheless be handled in socially acceptable ways through acquiring enough information about it, and practicing techniques of self-control; 4) an absorbing and confusing individual experience that gains immeasurably in intelligibility and enjoyment when it is shared with other pregnant women. The interplay of these four socialization processes to a great extent determines how a woman perceives and lives her pregnancy, what kind of birth she chooses to have, what kind of birth she actually does have (for the two are often radically dissimilar)--and will influence how she relates to and cares for her new baby and herself as a mother.

This article is based on data gathered in Austin, Texas; McAllen, Texas; and Chattanooga, Tennessee, from fifty women, most of whom are first-time mothers. I was a member of the group of pregnant women and new mothers which I studied in Austin, and I include myself among my informants. Because my anthropological observation was--for a time--also intense participation, my methods of data-collecting have varied from unadulterated social interaction later jotted down from memory, to more formal interviews with tape recorder or note-pad in hand. I interviewed pregnant women and mothers of young children wherever I found them--in my own group of friends, in the hospital after my daughter was born, on the streets, in restaurants, at parties, in their homes, in my classes, and one on an airplane. They are all white, urban, middle- to upper-middle-class mainstream women under 35, all of whom have or are getting college educations. I have been able to follow many of them through the entire process of pregnancy, birth, and early motherhood. The fact that I have been unable so far to include husbands and partners in my study more than peripherally is in no way intended to ignore or disparage the intense participation and involvement of many of these men in the pregnancy/childbirth process.

Although this is a limited sampling of American women, I feel that these data are important precisely because they reveal so many contradictions and conflicts between modern American medicine and the group of people whom it purports to serve best. As Brigitte Jordan reports in her study of birth in four cultures, in many cultures the practitioners of a birthing system see their system as "the best way, the right way, indeed *the* way to bring a child into the world" (1980: 2) and "in the United

States, in fact, the appropriateness of the medical model for the entire conception of birth has become questionable" *(Ibid:* 4). Like her, in this study I assume that "the practices and reasonings of American medical obstetrics [do not] provide an inherently superior standard for comparison" *(Ibid:* 90) with those others, including others within our own society such as midwives and the proponents of home birth.

However, all of my informants (and I, who am one of them) began their pregnancies assuming this very superiority of the American medical way of birth. I wish to stress that these women are products of the American medical system. They have been taught to delegate responsibility for their physiological--and especially their sexual and reproductive--functions to doctors, drugs, and medical technologies. Yet they all expressed some degree of "gut-level" discomfort with that socialization. Most especially they all felt a deep desire to make their pregnancies "natural," a term which of course can only have meaning in a culturally defined way (Jordan 1980: 97). For my informants, a "natural" pregnancy/childbirth seemed simply to mean one that was healthy, satisfying, and well integrated with their lives and their conceptions of self. Regarding the medical system of prenatal care in the doctor's office and hospital birth as "the only safe way to go," they did not wish to withdraw from participation in that system, but only to alter it enough to achieve their individual goals of a "natural" process of child-bearing and birth. Yet both American society and the medical profession treat pregnancy and childbirth so unnaturally that most of them were unable to achieve that goal.

In their well-planned efforts to create an individually satisfying rite of passage, many of these women won some battles with doctors on technical and scientific grounds, only to lose in the end to hospital ritual cloaked in scientific guise. Their experiences, as I have pieced them together and compared them with those written about by others, reveal both a system in conflict and the colossal efforts under way to reform it. I dedicate this paper to everyone involved in that effort (many of their works can be found in its bibliography), and I present these data as a contribution to it, in the hope that they may broaden our understanding of the cultural factors involved.

Pregnancy as a Rite of Passage

Pregnancy, birth, and the newborn phase of motherhood together constitute a single life-crisis rite of passage involving major changes of state and status for the woman. While birth has commonly been recognized by anthropologists as a rite of passage, the significance of the entire cycle of pregnancy through early motherhood *for the woman* has largely been ignored in studies of this society, even though it was pointed out in 1908 in Arnold van Gennep's seminal work on *Rites de Passage* (1966: 41-43).

Rites of passage, as van Gennep showed, are the elaborate mechanisms developed by cultures around the world for moving individuals from one social classification to another as they pass through the life cycle. They generally consist of three principal stages, outlined by van Gennep as 1) separation of the individuals involved from their preceding social state, 2) a period of transition in which they are neither one thing nor the other, 3) an integration phase in which through various rites of incorporation they are absorbed into their new social state. Van Gennep states that these three stages may be of varying degrees of importance, with rites of separation generally emphasized at funerals, and rites of incorporation at weddings. Yet the most salient feature of all rites of passage is their transitional nature, the fact that they always involve what Victor Turner (1969; 1972) has called "liminality," the stage of being betwixt and between, neither here nor there. For Turner, this liminal period is above all an anti-structural process of becoming, as opposed to a structural "state," in which one "is." The interesting thing about pregnancy viewed from a Turnerian perspective is that it is both a "state" *and* a "becoming." (Webster's gives the etymology of pregnant as L. *praegnans--prae* 'before,'' *gnans* "being born," and defines pregnancy as "the state of being pregnant." Translated literally, that would be "the state of being before being born.") Pregnancy's dual nature as a state and a becoming (for both woman and child) gives it both structural and anti-structural aspects.

Turner (1974) and Sutton-Smith (1972) view anti-structure as a free-flowing blending of forms and ideas between structural states, as the dip into unclassified chaos that can reinvigorate society's creaking classifications. Sutton-Smith states:

> The normative structure represents the working equilibrium; the anti-structure

> represents the latent system of potential alternatives from which novelty will arise . . . We might more correctly call this second system the *proto-structural* system because it is the precursor of innovative, normative forms. It is the source of new culture (1972: 18-19, quoted in Turner, 1974: 60).

But it was first, I must emphasize, the source of new life. In short, it seems to me that the physiological processes of pregnancy and birth are actually the models from which most of the characteristics of liminality and anti-structure are drawn. There is certainly nothing more proto-structural than the womb--worldwide, the dominant symbol for people in the process of rebirth. It is the generative, literal source of new culture, the "real thing," the baseline from which metaphor grows. This indeed is the heart and soul of our own Western Christian mythology--that life comes out of chaos, light out of dark.

If it seems strange to think of pregnancy as a kissing cousin of chaos, we need only recall that in our society pregnancy has but recently been accepted as appropriate to the public domain. Before World War II, pregnant women were examples of the structural invisibility of liminal personae (Turner 1972: 339)--very nearly as hedged about with ritual and taboo as Turner's Ndembu initiates. They were expected to remain secluded in their homes, as their presentation in public was somehow felt to be improper. When in public their pregnancy was to be disguised. Even the word "pregnant" was too pregnant to be used. Just as people did not die, but "went to sleep," or "passed away," pregnant women were "with child," "p.g.," "in the family way," "expecting," or "baking a bun in the oven." The mysterious procreative powers of nature, made undeniably manifest in the visibly pregnant woman, were too threatening to a society that wanted to believe it had ultimate control. These euphemisms helped to mask the fact that it is nature, not society, that controls the creation of new human beings. And the undeniable but highly anomalous fact that the pregnant woman, unlike all other human beings, holds two individuals in one body, presented absolute proof that, mathematics notwithstanding, two--or more--*can* come out of one, as in the act of childbirth each woman re-creates every culture's creation story.[1]

In the last two decades pregnancy, like homosexuality, has come out of the closet into a society now somewhat more inclined to celebrate than suppress nature--pregnancy has become a culturally recognized structural state. We see pregnant women everywhere, from the night club to the theater, and it is only a few old die-hards who mutter under their breath about unseemly display, or raise eyebrows at Loretta Lynn singing "Pregnant Again" on the Tonight Show. Yet, as the Ndembu youth, no longer boy and not yet man, is both sacred and contaminating to society, so the pregnant woman, neither one nor two, neither childless nor mother, public proof of a sexuality properly kept private, walking representative of nature in a culture that seeks to deny nature's power, still crosses too many categories for comfort![2]

Therefore it seems to me more than coincidental that concurrent with this rise to respectability has been pregnancy's near-total takeover by the medical profession. (In the U.S., 95 percent of all babies are born in hospitals.) As doctors have moved the rites and rituals of pregnancy and childbirth from the tutelage of midwives and the domain of the home (Arms 1979; Ehrenreich and English 1973) into the (supposedly) sterilized insulation of their offices and hospitals, thereby announcing to society at large that these forces of nature are now "under control," society has gradually lost some of its fear of them. Yet, though accepted as a state, as a becoming pregnancy is still taboo-laden and ritually hedged, although now many of the taboos are cast as medical necessities, and many rituals are thought of as scientific or educational procedures pertaining to the state. In other words, I suggest that pregnancy's recent rise to status and respectability serves to mask and disguise the still forceful cultural perception of it as a ritual process. I will have more to say about this later on.

As we have seen, the most cross-culturally prominent types of rites of passage are those dealing with life-crises. They accompany what Lloyd Warner has called

> the movement of a man through his lifetime, from a fixed placental placement within his mother's womb to his death and ultimate fixed point of his tomb-stone . . . punctuated by a number of critical moments of transition which all societies ritualize and publicly mark with suitable observances to impress the significance of the individual and the group on living members of the community. These

> are the important times of birth, puberty, marriage, and death (1959: 303).

The sequence of these life-crisis events which Warner uses is the traditional one; in this sequence, birth by its placement at the beginning must refer to the baby's birth, and not the woman's giving birth nor her transition into motherhood. Thus this sequence reveals a strong male bias which may be a reason for the general anthropological overlooking of the extreme significance of the rites of pregnancy/childbirth in this culture. Arranged from a female-oriented physiological perspective, the sequence would have to read: birth, puberty, marriage, child-bearing, menopause, death.

In the following section I will attempt to get at the significance of this overlooked life-crisis rite of passage for the woman in American society, and at the significance of its takeover by the medical profession. I will very briefly discuss each of the three stages--separation, transition, and integration--of this rite of passage, in order: 1) to demonstrate *in vivo* why I consider the three seemingly separate events of pregnancy, birth, and the newborn phase of motherhood to be parts of one single rite of passage;[3] 2) to demonstrate the significance of this oneness for the pregnant woman, namely, that during birth she is at the most intensely liminal and sacred--and therefore at once powerful and vulnerable--phase of the rite; and 3) to demonstrate the intimacy of the relationship between this rite and the medical profession. Later on I will discuss the unsettling effects of that relationship, and the processes through which women are socialized into accepting those effects.

Phase I: Separation

Van Gennep states:

> The ceremonies of pregnancy and childbirth together generally constitute a whole. Often the first rites performed separate the pregnant woman from society . . . they are followed by rites pertaining to pregnancy itself, which is a transitional period. Finally come the rites of childbirth intended to reintegrate the woman into groups to which she previously belonged, or to establish her new position in society as a mother, especially

> if she has given birth to her first child . . . the return to ordinary life is rarely made all at once; it, too, is accomplished in stages reminiscent of initiation steps. Thus the mother's transitional period continues beyond the moment of delivery, and its duration varies among different peoples. The first transitional period of childhood . . . is grafted to its latter stages (1966: 41-43).

For the newly pregnant woman, this phase of separation from her former social--and personal--identity usually begins as an intensely personal experience, when she first starts to suspect that perhaps she is pregnant. She will probably live with the wondering for a time; finally, wary of misinterpreting what her body tells her, she will usually seek first the scientific confirmation of the drugstore test. If the results convince her, her next moves will usually be to tell the baby's father and call the doctor--in reversible order. If the test does not convince her, she will see the doctor anyway to obtain a final answer. From that day on, she will mark the process of her pregnancy in routine monthly visits to the obstetrician. She will know her baby is alive when she hears its heartbeat on the monitor. She will tell the doctor when she first feels it move, and he will tell her that she is now half-way through the pregnancy. She will eagerly await the due date he sets using his standardized chart or formula, even if she is fairly sure that the baby was not conceived when the chart says it must have been. If the "due date" comes and goes with no sign from the baby, she will grow increasingly anxious with each passing day in which she does not conform to medical expectation.

Meanwhile, in the private domain of her relationship to herself, her first days of beyond-a-doubt pregnancy will be ones of inner turmoil--maybe excitement, maybe anguish, certainly some panic and much self-questioning. Already her conception of self is being tested--her body is doing things on its own, and she must cope with its changes and her total lack of control over them. By the time she has fully accepted the fact of her pregnancy and gone public with the news, neither she nor those close to her will see her quite as they did before. Already at least three of the four socialization processes I discuss in the next section have begun to operate, as her friends begin to symbolize her, as she begins to develop an understanding of what is happening to her body, and as her doctor begins to medicalize those natural events. The socialization processes that accompany her progress through this rite of passage are discussed in detail in the second part of this paper. In this brief summary of the phases of this rite of passage to motherhood, I seek only to indicate the general outlines and most salient characteristics that were common to the experiences of all my informants.

Phase II: Transition

What Turner calls liminality, we pregnant women experienced as a sense of change, of growth, of detachment, fear, wonder, awe, curiosity, hope, specialness, simultaneous alienation from and closeness to ourselves and our lives, irritation, frustration, exhaustion, resentment, joy--and a trembling sense of unknown, unknowable potentiality--all of which remained generally unaffected by our monthly forays into the medical realm. To all of that, the actual process of giving birth to our children added an extraordinarily heightened and intensified atmosphere and a near-total inward focus as we either struggled or flowed with the powerful sensations of labor--as well as an extreme sensitivity to any irrelevant outside events that forced themselves through the delicate cocoon that formed around the outer edges of our circle of consciousness and concentration. This cocoon, of course, could not possibly remain unaffected by the medical realm in which, for most of us, it was formed. As is characteristic of liminal experiences around the world, after the birth was long over the feel and flavor of this experience remained indelibly imprinted on our minds.

To that feel and flavor, the days immediately following the birth added a whole spectrum of new emotions stemming from each individual's birth experience--like pain and anger, or despair and bitterness, bewilderment, or triumph, or relief and joy. Suffused with these emotional rainbows, these first newborn days were passed in partial seclusion in a hospital or at home, while to the rainbow were added whatever emotions the new baby aroused in us, along with the flowers, the gifts, and the ritual congratulations of friends.

Even after those of us who had been in the hospital returned home and the festivities were over, all of us remained in partial seclusion with our newborns for some length of time, sometimes glowing, sometimes trembling, as we absorbed the impact of our experiences and the new sets of meanings associated with it.

Phase III: Integration

The final integrative phase of this rite of passage begins and ends sometime during the newborn's first year of life. Some women experience it as "post-partum depression," when the reality of the structural outside world begins to invade and dispel the special magic circle surrounding the mother and child.[4] (If the mother's birth experience has been a negative one, this depression will usually be considerably deeper and longer-lasting, as she attempts to re-work, re-interpret, and make some kind of structural sense out of what happened to her. See Peterson and Mehl 1977, Davis-Floyd 1986b: 329-347; and below.) Others experience it as a series of successful minor encounters with the outside world--like the first trip to the supermarket, to church, to class or the restaurant with baby-in-arm, in back- or front-pack, carriage, or stroller. At some point we all realized that we no longer felt trembly or potential, but mundane; our sense of special separateness was gone and we were mainstreaming it again. One informant said she had a strong sensation of "swimming up the other side." Some of us went back to work; others stayed home; others strove to do both. But in any case our change in state was complete; whatever else we might be, we were finally and completely mothers.

Pregnancy and Socialization

Women involved in this year-long rite of passage I have just outlined must cope with four often conflicting and contradictory views of pregnancy, each of which has a socialization process all its own through which she must proceed. I want to make clear that what led me to consider socialization in the first place was observing for myself these contradictions in the system. As I entered the community of mothers, I met woman after woman who, like myself, looked forward eagerly to a fulfilling and joyful childbirth, who prepared themselves thoroughly for that experience, who believed in the possibility of having their expectations fulfilled, and who were ultimately disappointed by their inability to achieve that goal. Each one of these women has spent countless hours trying to sort through her bewilderment and sense of failure to find out where she went wrong.

I began to ask the question, first for myself and then for others as well; why is there such disparity between the need and the actuality? I have found part of that answer in the realization that pregnancy is a rite of passage whose purpose for the individual woman is supposed to be transformative, but whose transformative power is often weakened or lost in the clash between the woman's needs and the medical profession's denial of them. I found another part in the confusion of our cultural perceptions of pregnancy, and in the means by which these confused perceptions are transmitted to the pregnant woman. I found that this culture does still treat pregnancy as a ritual process. Rituals are patterned, repetitive, symbolic, and transformative. Anthropology tells us that any powerfully transformative ritual will be protected by social boundaries and laden with regulation and taboo (Turner 1964; Douglas 1966). Pregnancy is not only socially but also physically transformative, and it transforms in several senses: it makes a woman a mother, a fetus a person, and one being into two--so it is triply powerful and will therefore be dealt with by society in highly symbolic, ritualistic, protective, "hands-off' ways. How this happens in our middle-class society will be discussed immediately below. The spilling over of this cultural perception of pregnancy as a ritual process into the medical domain will be discussed in the following section on pregnancy as a medical event, as well as the socialization of both women and doctors to this medical view of pregnancy. The next section treats the educative process through which women come to view pregnancy as a "natural" process, and will attempt to demonstrate the results of the clash between the "natural" and medical definitions of pregnancy, both of which are heavily influenced by its ritual treatment. The final section, on pregnancy as shared experience, will look at the relationships developed by pregnant women with others in the same state of liminality--at how they socialize each other, often in balanced opposition to the preceding three socialization processes whose effects they all feel.

Pregnancy as a Ritual Process:
Socialization through Symbols

> "What do you mean, Earth Mother? I'm no Earth Mother, I'm Melissa!"

Turner stresses that an important aspect of liminal phenomena is that their symbols tend to have common intellectual and emotional meanings for all members of a given group; they are multi-vocal powerhouses of emotional energy and storehouses of information (Turner 1968: 2). It was a common experience of all my informants that in the public domain, the visible physical fact of their pregnancy frequently turned them into objects, specifically symbols, for their friends, and for strangers both female and male.

All found that their symbolic transformation was sometimes negative. Some men, formerly friendly, began to avoid them as their bellies grew, occasionally admitting openly that the big stomach embarrassed them. Some women found that people talked to them while staring at their stomachs instead of their faces, thus increasing their sense of being made into objects. Sometimes it was other women who withdrew, perhaps viewing the pregnant one as a symbol of female subjugation by males or as a slave to her own body and to the forces of nature.

Common positive experiences were of being viewed as: Nature Personified, as the Venus of Willendorf (i.e., as a fertility symbol), as Earth Mother, Mother Nature, or as representing Motherhood or Womanhood, or the Creative Force at work in the universe, the Future, the Continuation of Mankind, the mystical union of the male/female principles, Yin and Yang, the Oneness of Man. Many of my informants eventually came to perceive themselves in one or another of these ways.

Reinforcing these perceptions was the behavior of men (and sometimes other women) in public places, who rushed to open doors and pick up dropped coins, who toted suitcases across airports and gave up seats on the bus. Apparently pregnancy increases the force of the stereotype of the weak female, or at least combines it with the cultural taboo against women lifting and carrying heavy things. The combination seems to open the door to a chivalry nowadays oft-suppressed. To these sorts of ministrations, the barely showing pregnant woman may at first react with disgust and scorn. Pregnancy has not changed her one bit: "By God, I'm no weak female; I can carry my own suitcase, thank you!"

But by the seventh or eighth month, whether delighted or simply resigned, she has adapted. She probably no longer flinches when strangers reach out to pat her stomach, having learned and accepted the social fact that her belly is now actually part of the public domain. She regards with more sympathy those who avoid her--sometimes she would like to avoid herself! And she accepts her social symbolic transformation, for in her own eyes she has been transformed by bewilderingly real biological processes over which she has no control. Many of my informants found it very comforting to adopt and use the symbols thrust upon them as a framework within which to conceptualize and interpret their new physical realities. This process seemed to become an integral part of their rite of passage, of their separation from their former conceptions of self:[5]

> One thing that struck me was how, when pregnant, an aspect of taboo/liminal status was becoming, as it were, public property: in a shoe store, the saleswoman told me not to buy stack heels; hands-on-tummy; concern (don't reach, lift); then "your baby will get a cold if you don't put a hat on" when I was walking; comments/concern around my failure to observe the seclusion rule on return from the hospital . . . the "end" of it all was that loss of the public eye, the recognition that pregnant women no longer looked at me and my baby and smiled. [Michelle Rosaldo, personal correspondence, Sept. 15, 1981.]

Pregnancy as a Medical Event:
Socialization through Fear

> I really trusted my O.B. He was a warm and gentle man. When I asked him about a home birth, he looked at me gravely and said he would never deliver a baby at home because the risks were just too high. So we went to the brand new birthing center he had helped to start. It was really pretty--nice furniture, Halston sheets on the double bed. When the contractions started coming hard, I wanted to pace the halls, but the nurses made me lie down. After 12 hours of labor I was only two centimeters and the doctor wanted to put me on pitocin. He said it would help my cervix dilate. So they kicked us out of our nice room and escorted us down the hall to the big double doors of labor and delivery. It was like walking through the gates of hell. For the next five hours I was strapped to the fetal monitor, fed pitocin through the I.V., and checked for dilation by six different people. Every time Stan and I would get our breathing together and start flowing with the

> contractions, someone else would come in to stick their hands inside me or check the monitor. They broke my water with a long hook. Somebody tried to stick those electrodes into the baby's scalp, but we wouldn't let him. Then the doctor called from church to say he'd be there in an hour to do a C-section, because I still wasn't dilating. By the time he got there, we were too exhausted and defeated to argue.
>
> --Elizabeth

> It is very difficult for a person trained in technical know-how to do technically nothing during a normal birth.
>
> --Michael Whitt, M.D.
> (Arms 1977: 64)

In her recently published book, *Birth in Four Cultures*, Brigitte Jordan (1980) convincingly demonstrates the effect on the woman in childbirth of our culture's definition of birth as a medical event--a definition which stands in glaring contrast to birth as conceptualized in Holland and Sweden, both countries with two of the lowest infant mortality rates in the world. Jordan shows how in the hospital, laboring women are dehumanized, objectified and subjected to painful taboos and rituals, which are justified by the hospital staff as medically necessary, but which actually are the result of an overlapping or confusion of the science of medicine with what Jordan calls the "culture of doctoring" (1980: 73). In other words, in the hospital we see disturbing results of the conflicts in our cultural definitions of pregnancy and birth.

The laboring woman who allows herself to be stuck with an unnecessary I.V. needle, who lets her labor be speeded along with pitocin, and who endures the suddenly much intensified contractions lying flat on her back and strapped to a fetal monitor because "the doctor knows best" is at the end of a medical/mythological socialization process that renders all of us in America passive victims of American medicine, and herself triply so.[6]

For most of us this process of socialization into the mythology of medicine begins in childhood. In her sensitive study of children in hospitals, Ann Hill Beuf (1979) shows us that children who become patients are the victims of double jeopardy, expected on two counts--as children, and as patients--to be obedient, quiet, cooperative, undemanding objects, passively receiving what the hospital staff chooses to dole out. What they do dole out is itself totally governed by hospital routine, by the all-encompassing ambience of Goffman's "total institution" (1961).

I suggest that laboring women are in this same double bind--plus one. They have already been socialized to the patient role, probably as children. They have also been socialized as *women* to a chillingly similar role (Graebner, 1975), which emphasizes, as Anton Derber (1979) has pointed out in his recent study of attention, learning how to give more attention than they get, how not to create scenes, how to be "good." And third, they are in labor, an intensely liminal condition which itself demands almost total attention and concentration and therefore renders them extraordinarily vulnerable to external pressures. With those three counts against her, the consistent victimization of the American woman in childbirth by the medical establishment, as graphically reported by Jordan, Sheila Kitzinger (1978), Suzanne Arms (1979), Lester Hazell (1969, 1976), Adrienne Rich (1977), Robert Mendelsohn (1979, 1981), and others is hardly surprising. She has, although she does not know it, been prepped for it since her own birth.[7]

According to Beuf, children receive an early, if incomplete model of what to expect in a total institution in school, a place where one is generally regimented and "done to," and where one learns, as Goffman points out in *Asylums* (1961) to redefine one's sense of self in statistical, bureaucratic terms. Pregnant women have nine months of trips to the obstetrician's office as a refresher course in institutional self-perception; these visits establish the tone of things to come.

A brief example of my point should suffice, an excerpt from one informant's description of her first visit to the O.B.:

> They got me undressed; they laid me on the table and put my feet in the stirrups with a sheet over my knees [I'm sure we all recognize the position!] and told me the doctor would be in in a minute. After they left the room, I sat up. When one of the nurses came back in, she said, "You sat back up!" I said, "I'm not about to meet a doctor lying down!"

Although this obstetrician had been recommended to my informant as one who favored "natural childbirth," by the end of the interview she conducted, sitting up, he had 1) tried to treat her like a child by brushing aside her questions ("Trust me, dear"); 2) demonstrated to her watchful eye a confusion of terms and a conflict in values. In my terms, he wavered between the medical and natural definitions of childbirth; e.g., "I believe in letting mother nature take its course" vs. "No, I would not consider delivering you at home; too many things could go wrong."

Of course, it is precisely this argument--the citing of all that could possibly go wrong, or the real clincher, "Do you want to risk losing your baby?" that many obstetricians use to scare women into having their babies in the hospital (Mendelsohn 1981). The amazing fact is that there is much evidence that suggests there is more risk involved in having a baby in the hospital than at home.

Dangerous Lifesavers:
The Ritual Use of Medical Technology

> The first problem associated with hospital delivery is the hospital itself. The conservative estimate of iatrogenic [doctor-induced] disease developing after hospital admission is 25 percent . . . The rate of iatrogenic disease among obstetrical patients . . . approaches 100 percent (Birnbaum, 1977: 105-106).

> "It's a wonder you didn't get an infection, with so many people sticking their hands up inside you," said Elizabeth's obstetrician to her one month after the birth of her child.

Much of my argument in this section on pregnancy as a medical event rests on a conviction that I have come to after interviewing not only pregnant women and mothers, but also doctors, nurses and other hospital personnel--and after reading a number of books, including medical textbooks. This conviction is that most of the procedures that are standard to most hospital deliveries in the United States are medically unnecessary and scientifically unjustifiable; instead of the truly logical cause-and-effect procedures they are purported to be, from the shaving of pubic hair to the structural alteration of the vagina, these procedures are the ritual means by which the hospital personnel mark the management of the birthing process as exclusively their own, claiming any attendant transformative energy for themselves (see below, pp. 45-46). Were these procedures truly justifiable on medical grounds, I would have little to say in this section beyond showing their sometimes devastating effect on the laboring woman's mind and emotions, while citing their physical efficacy as well worth the price. There would be little to say anthropologically about doctors themselves, beyond perhaps a look at how they view themselves as gods for certifiable reasons, or explication of the technical means by which they transform an extraordinarily dangerous process into a safe and successful one.

But I have more than that to do here, for the processes of pregnancy and birth in the vast majority of cases are not life-threatening, while the techniques and procedures doctors use to intervene in this process--under guise of making it safer--are themselves at worst life-threatening and at best potentially dangerous to both mother and child if misused. The fact that these procedures are so commonly used across America reflects something other than a true concern for the pregnant woman's health and safe delivery of her child. Fortunately, the burden of proof for these statements does not rest with me. The case has already been thoroughly discussed and documented in a number of works (Arms 1979, Brewer and Brewer 1977, Feldman 1978, Jordan 1980, Mendelsohn 1979, 1981, Parfitt 1980, Stewart and Stewart 1976, 1977, 1979, 1981; Inch 1984; Brackbill, Rice and Young 1984). Many of their findings, I can add, are borne out in the experiences of my informants. Yet because my observations that the influence of doctors on the birthing process is often more harmful than beneficial, more ritualistic and more reflective of the values and world view of the medical profession than of legitimate aid to the woman, may seem radical and exaggerated to some of my readers, in this section I will provide documentation of the harmful effects and the ritualistic nature of a few of the procedures that are most commonly used to affect the childbirth processes of many of my informants. These include the use of the lithotomy (flat-on-your-back) position for labor and delivery, the artificial stimulation of labor with the hormone oxytocin, the routine insertion of the intravenous needle, the use of both internal and external fetal monitors during labor, and the routine episiotomy.

Other risks which I will not discuss here have filled other volumes. These run the gamut from well-documented dangers to the fetus from pain-killing drugs (Birnbaum 1977) to the extraordinarily frequent and equally dangerous American Cesarean section. Parfitt asks, "Why is the Cesarean rate in this country and Canada approaching 25 percent, higher than anywhere else in the world?" (1980: 97) In some hospitals, especially teaching hospitals, it goes as high as 50 percent. By contrast, in Holland--where most babies are delivered by midwives--it is around 4 percent (Arms 1979: 97; Parfitt 1980: 97). A partial answer to Parfitt's question is to be found in the end results of some of the "medical" practices discussed below. (See Davis-Floyd 1986b: 183-185. The reader may discover another clue in the findings of a recent survey: the vast majority of C-sections performed in this country are done between the hours of 10 a.m. and 4 p.m.; Stewart and Stewart 1977.)

When a woman in labor enters the hospital, she is checked for cervical dilation and regularity of contractions; her pubic area is shaved (more modern facilities now only clip, an acknowledgement that this procedure is for the staff's convenience only); she may be given an enema, and she is put to bed. If she is in a modern birthing center within a hospital, she may be allowed to move around freely for a good part of her labor, but in most cases she will eventually be encouraged to lie down. Concerning this position, Roberto Caldeyro-Barcia, M.D. and President of the International Federation of Gynecologists and Obstetricians, said: "Except for being hanged by the feet, the supine position (lying flat on one's back) is the worst conceivable position for labor and delivery" (quoted in Ettner 1977: 149). Doris Haire (1972) succinctly summed up the reasons behind Caldeyro-Barcia's statement by showing that the flat-on-your-back position of American childbirth tends to:

1. adversely affect the mother's blood pressure, cardiac return and pulmonary ventilation;
2. decrease the normal intensity of the contractions;
3. inhibit the mother's voluntary efforts to push her baby out spontaneously;
4. increase the need for forceps and increase the traction necessary for a forceps extraction;
5. inhibit the spontaneous expulsion of the placenta which in turn increases the need for cord traction, expression or manual removal of the placenta--procedures which significantly increase the incidence of fetomaternal hemorrhage;

6. increase the need for episiotomy because of the increased tension on the pelvic floor and the stretching of the perineal tissue. The normal separation of the feet for natural expulsion is about 15 to 16 inches, or 38 to 41 centimeters, which is far less separation than is allowed by the average American delivery table stirrups (quoted in Arms 1979: 104).

In spite of all this, doctors and hospital staffs continue to either require or encourage women to lie down, for (I believe) several reasons: 1) The conceptual system of the hospital staff, which equates sick people with bed, the hospital with sick people, and laboring women, because they are in the hospital, with both. 2) The fact that this supine position greatly facilitates any actions that the hospital staff may want to perform upon the laboring woman, from insertion of the intravenous needle, to attachment of the fetal monitor, to frequent (and often painful) checks for cervical dilation, to the slicing open of the woman's vagina (episiotomy) by the doctor as he delivers the baby. In fact, it is this position more than anything else which insures that the doctor, not the woman, will deliver the child. For it has been shown (Haire 1972; Ettner 1977; Mehl 1977) that the contractions of the laboring woman are much more effective in causing the cervix to dilate when she is standing, sitting or walking than when she is lying down, and that the delivery itself is much more easily accomplished from a squatting, sitting, or kneeling position.[8]

When, as often happens, the laboring woman's cervix is not dilating as rapidly as the doctor believes it should (in medical school he is taught a definite timetable for each stage of labor; see Niswander 1976: 236; Wynn 1979: 66), although studies of home birth show that each of these stages when not interfered with can vary widely in duration while still resulting in normal deliveries (Mehl 1977), the doctor will usually elect to artificially stimulate labor with pitocin, the standard version of the natural contraction-regulating hormone oxytocin. Jordan (1980: 44) describes how pitocin is often administered in the hospital because of the social interactional awkwardness that results when the medical delivery room team shows up gowned and gloved and ready for action, yet the woman's labor slows down. The team members stand around awkwardly until someone finally says, "Let's get this show on the road!"

In an article on doctor-induced damages to mother and fetus, Frederic Ettner describes some of the dangers involved in the artificial stimulation of labor:

> Dr. Roberto Caldeyro-Barcia has demonstrated that uterine contractions stimulated with pitocin reach over 40 mm Hg pressure on the fetal head. The quality and quantity of uterine contractions are greatly affected when oxytocin is infused. The contractions tend to be stronger, longer and with shorter relaxation periods between. As a result, the fetus is compromised--stressed, before its first breath. The rapidity and strength of contractions decrease the ability of the fetus to restore its supply of oxygen. With each uterine contraction, blood supply to the uterus is temporarily shut off. If deprived of blood supply, a fetal bradycardia (decreased fetal heart rate-deceleration) follows with oxygen deprivation and cerebral ischemia causing the grave possibility of neurological sequellae. Truly the fetus has been challenged, and the EFM [external fetal monitor] dutifully records the stressed fetal heart rate. With suspicions confirmed, a diagnosis of fetal distress is noted and elective Cesarean section is the treatment of choice (Ettner 1977: 153).

Not only do these "stronger, longer" pitocin-stimulated contractions stress the fetus, but also the mother; in their intensity and the rapidity with which they appear, they are much harder to cope with than the slow build-up of normal contractions (Arms 1979; Parfitt 1980). This is but one more extremely trying addition to the tremendous stress of the hospital environment itself; Newton (1977) reports that experiments with mice and other animals have shown that outside stress on the female during labor can severely retard the process of labor and often result in birth defects or other damages to mother and child. The doctor may also use pitocin to induce labor if he believes that the baby is overdue. An added danger here is that he may miscalculate the due date and thus cause the baby to be born prematurely.

In most American hospitals, it is standard procedure to insert an intravenous needle into the laboring woman. The medical justifications are threefold: 1) The intravenous fluids provide nourishment in lieu of the food that the laboring woman supposedly cannot digest. However, the "nourishment" is in the form of calories, not protein, and so eventually creates a negative nitrogen balance in the woman's body--a "condition of starvation" (Birnbaum 1977: 107). 2) The IV keeps a vein open and ready for the quick administration of analgesics and of oxytocin/pitocin--that is, it greatly facilitates medical intervention in the labor process. 3) Should the woman hemorrhage severely after delivery, her veins will collapse, making it nearly impossible to insert an IV needle for a blood transfusion. According to Benson's *Handbook of Obstetrics and Gynecology*, although post-partal hemorrhage is the "major cause of maternal deaths in the USA," it occurs with varying severity in only "5 to 8 percent of all patients delivered at term"; of these, in only about 2 percent of cases is the bleeding severe enough to require "surgery and blood replacement" (Benson 1980: 210). Benson implies that in a good many of these cases the hemorrhage is doctor-induced, as a result of faulty use of instruments or "mismanagement of the third stage of labor" (*Ibid.*), an implication supported in Williams' *Obstetrics* (Pritchard and MacDonald 1980: 878). Moreover, should post-partum hemorrhage occur as a result of uterine atony (failure of the uterus to contract), pitocin can be injected into the vein without necessitating an IV. In the frequent citing of the dangers of post-partal hemorrhage as a justification for sticking IV's into *all* laboring women, we have a classic case of medical overkill, of "'just-in-case' hospital obstetrics" (Ettner 1977: 152).[9]

Whatever the scientific justification, the ritual administering of the IV in practice serves the hospital's purposes well, by confining the laboring woman to her bed--where all good patients should be--and severely limiting her movements. (If she does choose to walk around, she must drag the IV apparatus with her.) It transforms her from an independent entity into one dependent on the hospital; the needle, the tape that holds it in place, the cord going up to the plastic bag hanging on the metal pole--all these function as signifiers (to both the laboring couple and to the hospital staff) of that dependence. For these reasons, as an anthropologist I am forced to interpret the IV as a ritual artifact whose functions in most cases are primarily communicative and symbolic, not "scientific." The IV, in short, becomes the laboring woman's umbilical cord to the hospital: as the babe in her womb depends on her for its nourishment, so is she now dependent on the institution for hers.

Another technological device which lends itself to this sort of interpretation is the electronic fetal heart monitor. The external monitor involves the strapping of a belt around the mother's abdomen, which records on a small machine both uterine contractions and the fetal heartbeat. The internal monitor, while more accurate and precise, involves screwing or clipping electrodes into the baby's scalp. These monitors are widely hailed by doctors as life-saving; when used correctly, in cases of real need for a close watch on the heartbeat, they often are. Yet their extensive and growing use during normal labors has created a whole new set of dangers: 1) They literally imprison the woman in the lithotomy position, which as we have seen creates its own dangers to the fetus. 2) Their proper interpretation requires a specialist (Parfitt 1980: 94), yet often they are used with none present; this may be one of the reasons for their high rate of inaccuracy (44 to 63 percent; Mendelsohn, 1981) which often leads to incorrect diagnoses and unnecessary C-sections. According to Dr. Alfred B. Havercamp, head of the high-risk obstetrics section at Denver General Hospital, "the use of internal fetal monitors nearly doubled the number of Cesarean sections performed in American hospitals between 1971 and 1976"--a use which, he continues, "has not improved the infant mortality rate, infant performance on the Apgar test, or the infants' neurological condition" (quoted in Mendelsohn 1981: 162-163). 3) This inaccuracy rate can work both ways: the physician who relies exclusively on the monitor may fail to pick up other signals that would indicate the need for an emergency Cesarean. While a special stethoscope to monitor the heartbeat is quite adequate for normal labors (Parfitt 1980: 94), its use requires a hands-on approach that does not allow the doctor the paper graph and thus the technological distance from the patient which the monitors provide. Rebecca Parfitt states:

> A Dutch obstetrician reported to Suzanne Arms that the machines were put away when it was realized that the mothers were receiving much less personal attention since the coming of the monitors; henceforth, they were only to be used in cases of genuine medical need (1980: 96).

(See Ettner 1977, Arms 1979, and Parfitt 1980 for careful reviews of the different types of internal and external fetal monitors, their benefits and risks. Ettner concludes that in many cases internal fetal monitoring is actually the cause of "fetal distress" and of the high rate of uterine infection in monitored mothers [1977: 147-152].)

Nevertheless, in the US, both types of monitors continue to be widely used in hospital births. Like the IV, their true function is ritual and symbolic; these machines convey to the laboring woman the unmistakable message that she is dependent upon the superiority of technology both for her baby's safety and for her ability to give birth.

> As soon as I got hooked up to the monitor, all anyone did was stare at it. The nurses didn't even look at me anymore when they came into the room--they went straight to the monitor. I got the weirdest feeling that it was having the baby, not me.
>
> --Diana

Another telling difference between birthing practices in Europe and the United States involves the use of the episiotomy, an incision the doctor makes in the perineum just before the baby's head emerges. Parfitt (1980: 86) finds that "the number of births where an episiotomy is *medically* necessary is less than one out of seven. In American and Canadian hospital births, about six out of seven mothers undergo this procedure. In the Netherlands, 6 to 8 percent have episiotomies; in England, approximately 15 percent do." Standard justification in obstetrics texts (e.g., Benson 1980: 151-52) is the possibility of a jagged tear. Yet midwives find that the vaginal tissues will rarely tear if the final stages of labor are not officially speeded along, and that if a tear does occur, it is usually much smaller than would have been the doctor's cut, and heals much faster and less painfully (Parfitt 1980; Jordan 1980; Arms 1979; Mendelsohn 1981; Stewart and Stewart 1977). It seems to me that the doctors' idea that "a surgical incision can be repaired more successfully than a jagged tear" (Benson 1980: 152) has more to do with our culture's obsession with straight lines (Lee 1950; Dundes 1980) than anything else.

It should be noted that the procedures used by doctors to intervene in the birthing process are by no means confined to labor and delivery alone, but may be applied throughout the pregnancy at many points. From the ultrasound[10] to the risky amniocentesis (a very valuable tool when used for detecting chromosomal abnormalities in the fetus--Tray-Sachs disease, etc.--but this test, which can be dangerous, is often used simply to determine sex; it is now routinely recommended for all pregnant woman over 35; Rothman 1986), to strict orders not to gain more than 25 pounds,[11] to an arbitrary formula for selection of a due date which leads to further testing if the baby does not arrive "on time," doctors are provided with multiple ways to take control of the process of pregnancy in this country, even though well over 90 percent of all pregnancies are normal, and even though the evidence shows that many of the complications arising during hospital births *are the direct result of medical intervention* (Haire 1972; Arms 1979; Jordan 1980; Mendelsohn 1979, 1981; Peters and Mendelsohn 1977; Stewart and Stewart 1977, 1979, 1981; Newton 1977; Ettner 1977; Birnbaum 1977; Brackbill, Rice and Young 1984).

If my point in this section is correct--that many of the most common medical interventions in childbirth are ritual performances that have much more to do with the culture of doctoring than with the nature of birthing--then a look at midwife-attended and/or home-births should reveal a definite lack of both the procedures and the problems discussed above. Indeed it does. Brigitte Jordan reports:

> In an experimental project at a county hospital in California, two nurse-midwives handled most normal deliveries for three years. During that time, fetal deaths, stillbirths, prematurity rate and neonatal death rate dropped drastically, only to shoot back up when doctors took over again. At that point, prematurity rate increased by almost 50 percent and the neonatal mortality rate more than tripled (Levy et al. 1971). . . . The program was not extended because of opposition from the Council of the California Medical Association (Jordan 1980: 47).

In a recent study of 1046 home and 1046 hospital births (Mehl 1977) in which home/hospital couples were matched, couple by couple, for maternal age, parity, socioeconomic status, education, *and risk factors,* some of the results were as follows. In the hospital there was six times more fetal distress, five times higher incidence of maternal high blood pressure, 3.5 times more meconium staining, three times more post-hemorrhages. In the hospital 3.7 times as many babies required resuscitation, infection rates of the newborn were four times higher, and there were over thirty times more birth injuries. While neonatal and peristaltic death rates were essentially the same for both groups, Apgar scores (a measure of the physical well-being of the newborn) were significantly lower in the hospital group. Another significant difference was in length of labor; hospital labors were much shorter, which seemed to be due "to the tendency of the hospital practitioners to intervene to shorten labor" (Mehl 1977: 188).

Some Thoughts on the Socialization of Doctors and the "Culture of Doctoring"

> "Don't put your hand up," said Chanesohn. "When I lecture you can do that. There's just six of us here."
>
> "For the last ten years," I said, "I've worked in medical facilities. And there's one memory that just keeps coming back now. I'd be sitting talking with a patient, in would sweep twelve coats, grab the chart from my hand, never introduce themselves to me or the patient, discourse loudly over the bed in technical jargon as if they were dealing with a hunk of beef, then sweep out without a word. On to the next case. Always in a rush. I don't want to become that kind of doctor. And what's particularly strange to me is that the people in my class here don't seem that way at all. Perhaps a little competitive, but that's about all. So the question in my mind for the past two weeks has been, what's the hamburger machine that chops up nice kids and turns them into the doctors I got to know? I don't have a lot in the way of an answer yet, but I can see a couple of clues. One is starting off by not having weekends like everyone else, then moving on to continuous round-the-clock work shifts on the wards. Combine that with an isolated setting, intellectually and emotionally. Eight or ten years later, you emerge. You're in your thirties. You never really had your twenties. You realize you never had a youth. Everyone else did. But you didn't. So how do you start treating the cause of this

> irretrievable loss, the patient? You treat him angrily, bitterly. You resent your job, you resent sick people. Maybe you decide that the only thing you can get out of this ordeal is cash. (LeBaron 1981: 58)

Why do women submit themselves to these psychological and physical indignities and dangers? I have come to the conclusion that any consideration of the socialization process leading to all of the above must begin not with the teenager's first trip to the gynecologist, not with the child's first trip to the pediatrician, although the cumulative result of these visits is certainly, as Mendelsohn points out, the gradual instillation of the idea that our bodies are beyond our control or understanding, and that only Modern Science in the form of the doctor can cope with them (1979: 16).

The first step in this process seems to be the doctor's socialization in medical school.[12] Arms (1979), Mendelsohn (1979), and LeBaron (1981), among others, have described the deadening teaching of medical orthodoxy to medical students selected on the basis of their test scores and achievement motivations, not on the basis of their humanitarian concerns. The curriculum in almost all medical schools seems to stress the latest in drugs and interventionist technologies, with little or no consideration given to nutrition or the patients' responsibilities and rights to control over what happens to their bodies.

Consider the following quote from a popular book used for the teaching of obstetricians, *Obstetrics and Gynecology* (1974, quoted in Arms 1977: 77), "The very act of coming to the physician puts the patient in a parent-child relationship." Regarding the first pre-natal visit, the text states, "The physician notices whether the patient is reacting to the interview in a feminine way or whether she is domineering, demanding, masculine, and aggressive."

While lip service may be given to pregnancy as a natural process, and some respect accorded it as a rite of passage, at base it is taught in medical schools as an abnormality, a pathological condition in which the doctor's intervention at all possible stages is highly desirable. Since I have not yet been able to do the fieldwork in medical schools, this statement is based on interviews with obstetricians and my readings of obstetrical textbooks (Pritchard and MacDonald 1980; Wynn 1979; Benson 1980; Niswander 1976). In further support of it I offer the following excerpt from *Gentle Vengeance*, Charles

LeBaron's novelistic account of his first year at Harvard Medical School:

> Ritti [a professor] proceeded to explain episiotomy . . . Frank . . . asked if this kind of surgical intervention couldn't be avoided through the proper exercises by the mother before delivery. There was some scattered applause, mainly from the women. Ritti was in a bind, since it seems to be a tradition that anatomists and surgeons regard themselves as natural allies against physiologists and internists and all others who may doubt the healing power of the knife.
>
> Gesticulating with passion . . . he went on the attack, informing Frank that times had changed for women. They were no longer merely mothers, they had careers, hard, demanding careers, just like men.
>
> "This is not my field, but I tell you this, my young friend" Ritti said, jabbing a finger at Frank in the top row. "It is too much to ask a woman to work all day, then go back home and do your exercises! It is already hard to be pregnant and to work. If I were a woman, I would say, 'To hell with these exercises men think up for me!'" (1981: 195-196)

As Parfitt astutely observes, there is a wide spectrum of size and procedure among hospitals, yet it is generally true that "the larger the hospital and the more closely affiliated with medical student education, the higher are its rates of maternal and infant mortality . . . and the less likely it is that you will be able to secure deviations from routine procedures" (1980: 138). This situation is due to the combination of three factors: 1) Medical students are usually required to learn straight medical orthodoxy, which allows little room for flexibility and innovation (Mendelsohn 1979, 1981). 2) There is usually a greater number of high-risk patients, often of low socioeconomic status, in these hospitals (Wynn 1979: 121). 3) Medical students need to practice the interventionist techniques they are being taught (Mendelsohn 1979, 1981).

In the written account of his daughter's delivery (1974; given to me by Sheila Richardson, a 10-year certified instructor of the Lamaze method in Charioteers, Virginia), Richard (no last name was indicated), himself an M.D., provides a good deal of insight into the teaching hospital birth:

> I am a medical doctor, now three years out of medical school, and have personally delivered 20-30 infants. This experience was gained at large urban, ghetto hospitals in Cleveland, Ohio. I cannot now imagine a human experience that is more distorted and perverted than pregnancy and delivery is for the frightened, uninformed, uncomforted ghetto woman giving birth in our coldly efficient, academic centers. In the black-humor system so often erected by defensive medical people, we classified laboring women in various ways: the "moaners," the "OH me'ers," the "dear Lord Jesus, help me'ers," and the most feared of all, the outright "screamers." Most women I saw were unmarried, did not want the child, and feared the birth experience as a great painful ordeal. It was just taken for granted by the medical students and staff that labor was an inevitable ordeal for all concerned, and the medical students were interested in mainly "complications" so that they could learn something or in big perineal lacerations so they could get to practice their suturing techniques. It seemed that prepartum education of the mothers had simply never occurred to anyone from the medical establishment, and innocent medical students, though sensing that something was wrong, usually fell into accepting the stereotypes of labor and delivery as a curse on womankind.
>
> I sketch this negative picture partly as an apology for the occasional lack of understanding Lamaze couples receive from obstetricians and staff people of OB services. Most, if not all obstetricians have received a majority of their experiences in harsh, indifferent environments similar to the one I have described. There was a set, established routine for doing things, usually for the convenience of the physician and nurses, and the laboring woman was someone you worked around rather than with . . .

> [My first] Lamaze delivery was one in which I assisted an OB intern because the private OB was too late. The image of that lady "pant-pant-blowing," joyfully pushing her baby into the world supported by her sweating, joyful husband remains as one of my most vivid medical memories, and I shall treasure always these moments as an entire room of doctors, nurses, and parents stood around laughing, shaking hands, with tears streaming down every face, my own included.

As Brigitte Jordan (1980: 73) points out, doctors are not right or wrong in any simple way. Although in general they favor the "standard package set of obstetrical practices"--with a number of outstanding exceptions, as Richard's report seems to indicate[13] --this position "must be understood as their unselfconscious participation in a consensual, culturally sanctioned system of practices which are grounded in the culture's definition of birth as a medical event." Here, Jordan continues, "we find ourselves in the fuzzy realm where the science of medicine shades into the culture of doctoring."

Within this culture of doctoring, and extending to many of the "patients" who willy-nilly become (albeit) a peripheral part of it, it seems to me that the doctor's mental conceptualization of himself and his profession is likely to be based on one or more of several basic metaphors: Medicine as Science, Medicine as Art, Medicine as Religion, Medicine as a Game of Strategy and Skill. (There may be many others, of course-e.g., medicine as theater, medicine as war.) Lakoff and Johnson (1980) have shown how the "metaphors we live by" can shape our perceptions of reality to the extent of actually defining reality for us (e.g., argument is war, love is a journey). If medicine is an art, then the doctor is the artist and the patient the plastic medium in/on which he performs. If medicine is a science, then the patient is a physically real object whose properties the physician/scientist seeks to understand, experiment with, and perhaps alter. If a game, then the doctor is the dealer who holds all the cards, and the patient's body is the board on which he plays them. If a religion, then the physician is either the high priest or God (and the nurses and orderlies angels and acolytes), and the pregnant patient is either penitent ("I just haven't been able to keep to that diet you prescribed!"), true believer ("my baby and I are alive today because of

Him!"), sacrificial victim ("Do with me what you will, Doctor!"), just-in-case agnostic ("I hate doctors and hospitals, but so many things could go wrong"), or out-and-out atheist ("Doctors are just rip-offs; I'm having this baby at home!").

I suggest the influence of these metaphors here only in the hopes of stimulating further research; I intend in so doing not to document but simply to suggest. One of the things I want to suggest is that all of these metaphors, while allowing little room for patients who do not perceive themselves in compatible ways, do have the advantage for the physician of allowing him a good deal of latitude. If the scientist's experiment fails, he can always try again. If the dealer loses the game, there are always others to be played. If the artist's painting doesn't sell, he can always put his brush to new canvas or find fresh clay to mold. If the high priest sins and repents, God will forgive his transgression (LeBaron notes somewhat cynically that the closer the medical student moves to actual patient care, the fewer seem to be the consequences of his mistakes; 1981: 236). But God Himself, of course, cannot fail--and it is perhaps in this metaphor that the physician, whose very human mistakes can cause so much non-metaphorical suffering and death, finds the greatest measure of comfort and security.

Anyone who has been around nurses is familiar with their common complaint against the physician, "He thinks he's God!" Leonard Stein provides some insight into how this god complex develops:

> For the physician a mistake leading to a serious consequence is intolerable, and any mistake reminds him of his vulnerability. There is little wonder that he becomes phobic. The classical way in which phobias are managed is to avoid the source of fear. Since it is impossible to avoid making some mistakes in an active practice of medicine, a substitute defensive maneuver is employed. The physician develops the belief that he is omnipotent and omniscient, and therefore incapable of making mistakes. This belief allows the phobic physician to actively engage in his practice rather than avoid it (Stein 1980: 171).

Robert Mendelsohn (1979, 1981), himself an M.D., explains how this belief of physicians in their own omnipotence has turned modern medicine into a full-fledged religion, in spite of the fact that it is still officially spoken of as a science. Pointing out that we put our faith in our doctors' knowledge and ability much as we do in God's, he shows how doctors have encouraged us to delegate full responsibility to them for our bodies and their functions just as we look to God to take care of any event over which we feel we have no control.

> When you fear something, you avoid it. You ignore it. You shy away from it. You pretend it doesn't exist. You let someone else worry about it. This is how the doctor takes over. We let him. We say: I *don't* want to have anything to do with this, my body and its problems. . ." (Mendelsohn 1979: 16).

Given our overall cultural attitude toward the body/nature, it makes perfect sense for doctors to be the high priests of pregnancy--which as we have seen is one of the most natural processes, and therefore as threatening and confusing as death--of which doctors (need I say it?) are also the high priests. Death and birth, the bases of our existence, have been dedicated to what Mendelsohn aptly names the Church of Modern Medicine.

To follow through a little further, it seems to me that some of the implications for the birthing process of the above-mentioned metaphor are as follows: if medicine is a science, then birth is a phenomenon of nature whose mechanisms and laws must be discovered; once these are established, any deviation from them is seen as "abnormal" and treated remedially. If the physician perceives his profession as an art, then he is the sculptor bringing life out of passive marble; both the beauty and the message are in the perfection of his chiseling technique ("Look at that incision! So clean!"); as a game, then the more babies he delivers, the higher his score and the higher he rates vis-à-vis the competition. (Think of medicine as theater, and the doctor is lead actor/director surrounded by supporting actors; the patient's body is the stage on which he performs.) Think of medicine in religious terms, and as high priest the doctor's presence sanctifies (= channels, controls) the otherwise chaotic and threatening process. Just as the Bororo shaman must ritually remove the raw vitality of organic matter from the hunter's meat before it can be eaten (Crocker 1985) and the orthodox Jew must salt out any trace of blood, so the doctor--society's representative--must ritually impose some form of social control on the raw forces of nature let loose in the physiology of birth. Through priestly mediation of the natural process, he makes it his (society's) own. As God, He makes it all happen: He creates, He delivers.

If, on the other hand, birth is not metaphorized, but treated as the autonomous physiological process that it is, then the *woman* is the conscious social agent who must cope with that process, and the doctor becomes a mere bystander, there only in case the process fails to proceed. At the ASPO (American Society for Psychoprophylaxis in Obstetrics) 1981 conference in Washington, D.C., Dr. Robert Howard (obstetrician at Hampton General Hospital, Hampton, Virginia) stated that in his efforts to return control of the pregnancy to the mother, the hardest thing for him to give up had been delivery of the child in the lithotomy position, in which he could put his hands on the baby as the mother pushed, move it around, try to ease it out. But if she squatted or knelt on all fours, *she* delivered, while he felt awkward because he had nothing to do but watch and wonder "What am I here for?" (Sheila Richardson, personal communication.)

Birth as a Liminal Experience:
The Neophyte and the Priest

> In hospital deliveries, responsibility and credit are clearly the physician's. This becomes visible in the handshake and "thank you" that resident and intern (or intern and medical student) exchange after birth. "Good work" is a compliment to the physician by somebody qualified to judge, namely another physician. Typically, nobody thanks the woman. In the common view, she has been delivered rather than given birth (Jordan 1980: 50).

That birth should be ritualized is neither surprise nor tragedy; it is everywhere treated in ritual ways, as Jordan points out in the quote with which I began this paper. That there should be specialists in managing the birthing process is also a cultural commonplace. That some of the power attendant upon birth, one of the two greatest transformative processes life provides (death is the other), should accrue to these specialists is also a phenomenon found across cultures (Jordan 1980; Ehrenreich and English 1973). Yet only in Western culture have the technological means been invented for transferring that transformative power in its totality to the specialist.

We have seen that pregnancy is a rite of passage, and that one of the chief characteristics of any rite of passage is its liminal, or transitional period. Let me once again draw the parallel between Victor Turner's Ndembu initiates and the liminal pregnant woman. Turner, more concerned with the autonomy of "well-marked and protracted marginal or liminal phases" (1972: 339) than with their linking functions (which reflect past states and foreshadow future ones) describes the unique characteristics of liminal personae or "threshold people." Some of these characteristics are that the neophytes "may be represented as possessing nothing, to demonstrate that as liminal beings they have no status, property, insignia, secular clothing indicating rank or role, position in a kinship system--in short, nothing that may distinguish them from their fellow neophytes. Their behavior is normally passive or humble; they must obey their instructors implicitly and accept arbitrary punishment without complaint (1969: 95). This apparent passivity is later revealed as "an absorption of powers which will become active after [the neophyte's] social status has been redefined in the aggregation rites" (Turner 1972: 343).

The role of the instructors (or elders, as they were called among the Ndembu whom Turner studied) is to impress upon the youths undergoing initiation into manhood "as a seal impresses wax" (Turner 1972: 343) the sacred knowledge about themselves and their universe that is felt to change their inmost being. Eliade describes initiation as:

> a body of rites and oral teachings whose purpose is to produce a decisive alteration in the religious and social status of the person to be initiated. In philosophical terms, initiation is equivalent to a basic change in existential condition; the novice emerges from his ordeal endowed with a totally different being from that which he possessed before his initiation; he has become *another* . . . Every primitive society possesses a consistent body of mythical traditions, a "conception of the world"; and it is this conception that is gradually revealed to the novice in the course of his initiation. What is involved is not simply instruction in the modern sense of the word. In order to become

> worthy of the sacred teaching, the novice must first be prepared spiritually. For what he learns concerning the world and human life does not constitute knowledge in the modern sense of the term, objective and compartmentalized information, subject to indefinite correction and addition (Eliade 1975: 27-28).

Instead, what the initiate learns constitutes the formation of a subjective inner state that is the result of the transformative rituals performed throughout the course of the initiatory rite of passage; these rituals produce "not a mere acquisition of knowledge, but a change in being" (Turner 1964: 343). I suggest that beyond the sensory deprivation, the making strangers out of families, and the very real physiological and psychological damage to mother and child that are the hallmarks of hospital birth, it is the denial by the elder/doctor to the woman of the possibility of this inner growth and transformation that most perverts and corrupts the American Way of Birth. Let me quote one of my informants:

> I was ten centimeters dilated and ready to push. I *walked* to the elevator, rode up to the delivery room, and climbed onto the delivery table. I was panting the whole time to keep the baby from coming out. I knew that I could time it exactly. I knew that I could do *anything*. I felt so powerful. I've never felt so powerful in all my life. I discovered an unbelievable strength and a total control in me that I never knew existed.

In contrast, the following is an excerpt from a female physician's account of a delivery which she was called to the hospital to attend because the woman's doctor had not arrived, although he had been called several times.

> I arrived in the delivery room. The patient, a seventeen year old, was doing well, mildly pushing, groaning, but not screaming. Nurses were saying anesthesia was on the way. I asked the patient if she had had any classes or preparation. She had not. I was looking forward to this delivery because the woman was in control. She had already successfully

labored many hours alone and I thought would enjoy the rest. The delivery itself, faced without panic, is far more rewarding, or more immediately rewarding, than the hours of laboring.

I gowned, gloved, checked her. She was fully dilated and would deliver quickly. I draped her according to patterns learned many years ago and repeated many times since. My hands always remember.

Then the anesthetist arrived--a young man, arrogant--and seated himself at her head. He placed a mask over her face and told her to breathe deeply. He reassured her it was almost all over. She had only two or three contractions to go. I asked him what he was giving her. He ignored my question. I knew he was ignoring me--it's one of those sexist moments. I was the "doctor in charge" but he was male. Minutes later he decided to answer, but I couldn't hear what he mumbled.

It didn't matter, though, because at that moment the obstetrician arrived. The anesthetist deepened her sleep to await the scrubbing and gowning of the OB. I stood at the perineum, disappointed I would be stepping out. The OB stepped in, ignoring my presence.

He and the anesthetist began to speak to each other. The patient was now choking on the tubes in her throat. Her labor had stopped; the table had been tilted further so the OB could look down on the spreading lips.

Then they spoke with contempt. The anesthetist saying angrily that the woman was gagging. The OB that she had stopped being any help to them--she wasn't pushing, her uterus wasn't contracting.

Forceps were unwrapped, applied, and with deepened anesthesia the infant was lifted up and out of his mother's womb by the iron clamps about his head. He was blue and listless, but soon recovered, with oxygen and some slapping.

The obstetrician and the anesthetist went on talking while the patient was sewn up. They spoke of partners, Puerto Rico, vacations, weather, etc. The event of birth was lost to standard male locker room talk. It was a standard American birth, but with one ironic loss. A student nurse had gone out to tell the family of the birth of a son. The doctor was angry. The nurse in charge was stern. It is the doctor's privilege to tell the family. It is part of the "delivery" to announce what he has delivered. His show had been stolen.

Much was lost in this delivery, though it is far from a bad one by our standards.

LOST:

1) This woman has now been reinforced in her belief that she could not birth herself, and that is a loss since she did so well for so many hours.

2) This woman and her family are now ever more grateful that the doctor arrived to remove the baby with forceps, since the patient couldn't deliver. They do not know that the need for forceps was created by the use of anesthesia.

3) This woman was treated with contempt while in a light state of anesthesia, and so was capable on some level of hearing.

4) This woman missed a chance to know her baby, touch and hear her baby at birth. They will already be strangers when she wakes.

5) This blue born infant ought to have been born pink and active. He had been sedated. We do not know what effects will be seen in his future.

6) This patient, her family, her child will all be grateful she delivered in a hospital where all this help was available (Harrison, 1977: 585-587).

Lloyd Warner (1959) states that the purpose of life-crisis rites of passage is "to impress the significance of the individual and the group on living members of the community" (1959: 303). I wish to stress here and throughout this paper that the "significance of the individual" that is impressed on the neophyte/pregnant woman by her elder/doctor is his own; what she is taught is that she has no significance. This she holds in common with the Ndembu initiates; they too must undergo ritual subjugation and humiliation at the hands of the all-powerful elders. But the transformed self-image with which they emerge is a positive one of increased knowledge, assurance, and independence. Unlike them, the new mother emerges from the birth imbued with the certainty that in the future she can care for neither her body nor her baby without the doctor's help.

Pregnancy as a "Natural Process"--
Socialization through Education

> I read the wrong books while I was pregnant. If I had read *Immaculate Deception* or the NAPSAC books, I would have delivered this baby at home with a midwife. But I believed my Lamaze teacher when she told me how wonderful the hospital's new birthing center was, that it would be just like home, only safer. What a joke!
>
> --Susan

Searching for the answers that the OB does not provide, all of my informants turned to books. As pregnancy has gained recognition as a state, these books have proliferated on bookstore shelves, with titles like *The Better Homes and Gardens New Baby Book* (Kiester and Kiester 1981) and *Prepared Childbirth* (Tucker and Bing).

Each stresses that pregnancy and birth are natural processes and that the more we know about them the better ours will be. At the same time they enumerate and describe in more or less detail everything that can possibly go wrong, together with the medical solution for it. In doing so, they too present mutually contradictory views of what pregnancy actually is.

While most of them seek to be as accurate and comprehensive as possible, so that the reader can choose what suits her from among the many kinds of birth they impartially describe, the cumulative effect seems to be the creation of an ideal image in the mind of the reader of what birth as a natural process *should be like*. The ideal stands at the top end of a downward moving spectrum of limited to extensive use of drugs and artificial aids, with the Cesarean section under general anesthesia at the bottom.

For my informants, a significant impression that the books create is that if a woman and her partner are well-enough informed, they will generally choose to have a "prepared natural childbirth," perhaps with some mild pain medication and the aid of an episiotomy--and, most importantly, *that the couple has the power to make this happen,* in spite of the doctor's conflicting conception of birth as a medical event. (Books that do not so mislead include Arms 1979, Brewer and Brewer 1977, Feldman 1978, Mendelsohn 1979, 1981, Parfitt 1980, Stewart and Stewart 1976, 1977, 1979, 1981; Kitzinger 1970; Brackbill, Rice and Young 1984; Inch 1984).

This impression fostered by the books we all avidly devoured is reinforced in the "prepared childbirth" classes. The charts and diagrams held up and interpreted by the Lamaze teacher, the breathing exercises she taught us, the "Lamaze bag" packed and ready in the trunk of the car--these gave us technical information and concrete techniques for sticking with the definition of pregnancy and childbirth we had by now all adopted as our own.

I regret to say that only 3 of my 50 informants felt that the act of giving birth actually fit their idealized definitions. These three gave birth at home surrounded, like Jordan's Yucatecans, by family and friends. Of the two who were "90 percent satisfied" with their hospital experiences, one had both husband and sister to run interference for her, and an extremely supportive obstetrician who was willing to wait out her 30 hours of hall-walking labor; and the other was only in labor for three hours. The fact is that the inherent contradictions in the socialization processes we undergo during our pregnancies cause them to fail totally to prepare us for the hospital interactional process, for several reasons: 1) Very few of the doctors, and very few of the books, acknowledge pregnancy as a ritual process. So, just as the books do not tell us that we will become symbols, the doctors and nurses either do not realize or will not admit the ritual nature of many of their standard procedures. 2) Nor do most of the books or doctors explain in advance the nature and reality of the passive patient role that accompanies the definition of birth as a medical event. These two facts result in head-on conflict with 3) The fact that the couple in question adheres to their definition of birth as a natural process which they are entitled to experience without interference, even though they are on hospital territory and are thereby placed at a tremendous interactional disadvantage and 4) This disadvantage is intensified by the fact that the couple would not *be* on hospital territory in the first place if they did not also share in the overall cultural definition of birth as a medical event. They are thus psychologically as well as interactionally at the mercy of the suggestions and strategies of the hospital staff.

Some of my informants were astonished to find that this situation often holds true even in the modern birthing center, which, as Jordan points out, is still hospital territory where "the woman still gives birth . . . attended by unfamiliar people [who retain] the real decision-making power. A guest on somebody else's turf with few rights and fewer resources, . . . [she] still does not own the birth" (1980: 35). These birthing centers are emerging in hospitals across the country as the medical profession's answer to the protests and demands of women scarred by their experiences in regular labor and delivery, and to the many sympathetic nurses and doctors who sincerely seek to provide something better. With their attractive decor, privacy, kitchenette, big double bed, and open door to family and friends, they seem to represent the perfect mediation of the home/hospital dilemma for many couples. Yet these centers only accept "low risk" women, so that a great many people are ineligible to use them. And "low-risk" can quickly become "high-risk" if the laboring woman's blood pressure should rise, or if she should fail to dilate in medically appropriate time, as Mendelsohn describes:

> Don't kid yourself into thinking that birthing rooms made up to look just like a real (motel) bedroom are going to make any difference. Once you allow yourself to be lured onto Modern Medicine's turf, they've got you. I have the recurring dream of a nice young couple going into the birthing room, like the one at Illinois Masonic Hospital--complete with brass bed and color TV set. The doctor smiles and acts just like a friendly uncle. But once the mother is strapped into the brass bed, the doctor pushes a button on a secret panel and the papered walls slide away, the furniture disappears, and they're suddenly in an operating room under the glare of the operating light with the surgeon standing there scalpel in hand ready to slice her belly from one end to the other. That fantasy isn't so unreal. Birthing rooms are not so isolated from the operating rooms that the brass bed can't be rolled into action before the young mother and

> father know what's going on. If you're on the doctor's turf, you play by the doctor's rules (Mendelsohn 1979: 139).

Most of my informants who started out in a birthing center ended up in labor and delivery.

So, if the labor is quick and easy, or if at least one member of the couple is able to recognize and maneuver among the four factors I have just discussed, or if the medical personnel are unusually cooperative, then they may be able to impose their natural process definition on the situation and make it stick. If not, their definition will lose ground in the course of the hospital interactional process to the combination of magic and science that we call modern medicine. Instead of the growth and self-discovery that are the purpose of initiation rites in so many other cultures, they will receive an affirmation of the *doctor's* value and indispensability, and a direct and stunning negation of their own.

**Pregnancy as Shared Experience--
Socialization through Stories**

> "What on earth is a Nuk nipple?
>
> --Helen

One day early in my pregnancy, it dawned on me that I was actually going to have a baby. Shortly after that I realized with a thud that I didn't know anything about babies, or about having them. And so I thought, well who is there to talk to who does know? And then I realized that I didn't even *know* anyone who had a baby.

At a party I discovered that a woman I had been introduced to had a two-year-old. As I confessed my fears and my sense of isolation, she smiled. "Don't worry," she laughed, "there's an underground network of mothers in this town, and you'll find it."

A few months later, Pam and I, both eight months pregnant, perched on the bed in my half-put-together nursery discussing the relative merits of Austin's two new birthing centers, and our respective obstetricians. Terms like cervical effacement, dilatation, and episiotomy flew between us as we firmed up our ideas about the sorts of births we expected to have. In the midst of our comparison of the hospitals' nursery facilities, Pam broke off to wonder of what possible use the left-over sink in her ex-kitchen nursery might be. We stared at each other blankly as the realization sank in that, although near experts on birth, we still knew absolutely nothing about babies.

Three months later we faced each other again, this time across an apartment clubhouse full of mothers and infants, debating the merits of cloth vs. disposable diapers, of Nuk vs. Gerber nipples and pacifiers, as another mother prepared to show us how to massage our tiny babies. Obviously, I had discovered the network.

Of course, there is a great deal of variation in the ways in which pregnant women in different cities get plugged into this "underground network." For most of us in Austin, it began with enrollment in an exercise class for pregnant women advertised at the Y. For my Chattanooga informants, it seems to happen primarily through church groups. For my informants in McAllen, Texas, a local swimming and tennis club was the catalyst. In any case, all of us found ourselves involved in the discovery of a new sub-culture.

It is no doubt indicative of American society's shift in this century from an extended to a nuclear family base that most of the women in these groups were first or second-time mothers with no network of near kin readily at hand to provide the socialization and support these women keenly felt they needed. And even when there were mothers, grandmothers, and aunts nearby, my informants tended to feel their advice and the stories of their childbirth experiences could not be of much practical benefit. My informants generally felt that they were modern women who had a much sounder base of new medical and nutritional information to rely on, and that their female relatives who most probably gave birth in technical ignorance or under general anesthesia could give them none of the information they were seeking.

Reinforcing these opinions held by my informants are the perceptions and attitudes of the older women themselves, who frequently seem to view their birth experiences as bewildering and embarrassing, and of little value to someone planning as courageous an adventure as having a baby without anesthesia. There also seems to be a dramatic difference in attitudes towards doctors, with older women being much less inclined to question or doubt their doctors' wisdom. I must stress that these are very general impressions, since I have not as yet been able to extend my research to include women over 35. I include these remarks in the hope that they will stimulate further research in this area. Another speculation of mine is that many women in their late twenties and thirties have grandmothers who did give birth at home and who breastfed their babies--all before the medical establishment displaced the midwives and ushered women into the hospital. To what extent are these grandmothers utilized as a source of information and support?

Victor Turner places great emphasis on the collective, shared nature of liminality. Once again I must draw the analogy with his Ndembu neophytes. Like them, we pregnant women were all suddenly confronted with drastic change in our lives and statuses. Equal in our inexperience, we searched together for the means to cope with this suddenly topsy-turvy world. That special, spontaneous, unity they shared, Turner calls *communitas* (1969, 1972). I felt it as a "secret sisterhood," Michelle as a "special sense of sharing." Janice said, "It's like belonging to a private little club"; and Dee put it this way, "Whenever I saw another pregnant woman, and our eyes met, I knew that she knew that I knew--y'know?--and we would smile. It felt good."

While the extent of this secret sisterhood as experienced by my informants seems to vary a great deal, it always seems to include all pregnant women encountered, both strangers and friends, and usually includes mothers of tiny infants as well. Some of us reported experiencing this sense of *communitas* also with mothers of young children, and a few reported feeling it for all women who had given birth, saying they felt their pregnancy placed them "on the other side" of womanhood in general.

Cultures get created and spread through language. I guess we knew that, for we talked to each other, as much and as long as we could. It became a common feature of our experience that two members of the sisterhood, even if mere chance-met strangers, would choose to discuss above all other topics the subjects of pregnancy, childbirth, and children, no matter who was there or what else was happening.

We rapidly learned the "pregnant people's getting acquainted ritual" that replaced the standard "Hello, who are you, and what do you do?" It goes like this: Look at belly, smile, raise eyes. "How many months are you?" "Seven." "Gosh, you don't look it." "I know, but I sure feel it." "I know what you mean. When is yours due?" "In April." "Do you care if it's a girl or a boy?" "What kind of delivery do you plan to have? Lamaze? Me too." "Who's your teacher?" "Who's your OB?" "Really? What do you think of him?"--and they're off.

What they're engaged in is far from idle talk. It is the serious business of socializing each other into the culture of shared pregnancy, which also means helping each other to prepare for the birth. Robin Ridington (1979) has shown how hunter-gatherers carry elaborate technological knowledge in their heads as pattern, code, artifice instead of artifact, and pass it on to others in story, symbol, and example. Just so do women encode their growing knowledge of pregnancy and childbirth in what Labov and Waletzky (1966) called "personal narratives"--especially and specifically narratives about the traumas of pregnancy, the giving of birth, and life with the newborn. As a network of mothers and mothers-to-be develops, these narratives, as one informant put it, become a part of the "repertory" of the group.

Encoded in them is a vast amount of information, which sometimes can serve to counterbalance the medical viewpoint of pregnancy and childbirth, as well as the educative ideal. "The doctor says you're too fat? Don't worry, Sybil gained 50 pounds and lost it all in two months. He said you can't go Lamaze if you develop toxemia? Well, Michelle did, and it worked out just fine."

Here we see the dialogue between the official and the informal. Encapsulated in these women's narratives is the information of actual experience that can be brought to bear on the issue at hand. Of them all, what I will call the childbirth narrative stands out as the most often used didactic and socializing technique. Interestingly, the form in which these childbirth narratives are most often told follows Susan Kalčik's isolation of the "kernel story" in her study of a women's rap group--that is, of a key phrase that identifies a particular story and brings its meanings and implications to the forefront of the group's consciousness--as illustrated in the title of her 1975 article, ". . . like Ann's gynecologist, or the time I was almost raped."

Although these stories as a women's speech genre constitute one of my chief research interests, there is very little space to consider them here. I will confine myself to a few short examples that I hope will illustrate both what the stories are like and how they function to counteract the influence of both the pathological and the idealized views of birth.

Darla's Story

When Darla had her baby nine years ago in Austin, she was one of the first to prepare for and insist on a more or less natural, untechnologically interfered with delivery in an Austin hospital. One of the things she most hated, and was most determined not to have, since she knew it was medically unnecessary, was an I.V. stuck in her hand--although she also knew it was standard hospital routine. Doing the breathing and handling the contractions well, she managed to convince three nurses in succession not to do it, until. . .

> this gray-haired *martinet* marches in the room with an IV needle in her hand. I said, "You get out of here with that thing. Don't you point that thing at me!" And she said, "Now dearie, we have to do this!" and she came at me with it. Well lucky for me it was between contractions. I was already 8 centimeters but I jumped off that labor table and I ran down the hall. I got as far as the elevator when I had another contraction, so I squatted down and breathed through it. Peter was standing there pleading with me to go back. "Where do you think you're going to go?" he said. "You can't leave!" I said, "Don't you let her stick that thing into me," and I wouldn't go back, just kept on breathing in the hall, until he promised to keep her away from me even if he had to use force. (Laughing) Well, it didn't seem funny then, but I guess it really was. I must have scared those people who got off that elevator to death.

For many of us in Darla's exercise class, this story told us a lot that the books and the doctors did not about the possibilities and the almost insuperable difficulties of triumphing over the fixed routines of a total institution. Because it was presented on one level as funny, we could face its unspoken agony on another. We kernalized it "Darla and the nurse with the IV." For Darla, this humorous kernel narrative had become the mechanism for filtering her at-the-time painful and chaotic experience into an acceptable structural framework. Through it we were able to share that experience and to translate it into a positive and realistic means of shaping our own. This story became especially important to those in exercise class because Darla was not only the class leader, but also one of the few already mothers in the group.[14] Its truth became apparent later, in our own hospital experiences, when we too with our husbands had to summarily dismiss an occasional bossy, overbearing nurse or overeager needle-bearing intern.

Most unfortunately, this kind of talk is all too often disparaged, by both men and women, as "women's talk," i.e. gossip. (Brigitte Jordan [1980: 98] notes, "A standard piece of advice contained in doctor's printed handouts for first-time mothers is to ignore what they might hear from other women. The labelling of women's knowledge as 'old wive's tales' contrasts it pejoratively with enlightened medical science.") And sadly, many of my informants seemed to feel that they were the ones who had failed, that it was somehow their fault. These people tell their stories over and over again, looking for clues to what went wrong, where, how, what should we have done differently? And others have triumphs over near disaster to relive and share.

Key "kept trying to squat during contractions, and the nurses kept grabbing me and turning me over on my back, until finally they strapped down my wrists and ankles. When they left, my husband cut the straps. . ." Linda had a "wonderful experience, except for one thing--well, it was just--they wouldn't let my husband be with me during transition, and that was when I needed him most. . ." Michele was breathing slowly and evenly through her contractions,

> and I felt so peaceful between each one. I didn't want to lose that. The doctor was concerned because I had a mild case of toxemia, and wanted to do a C-section. I looked straight at him in the middle of a contraction, and I gathered all the strength I had, and I said in a very calm and even voice, "I'm just fine." I kept remembering what had happened to Elizabeth, and I was not going to let that happen to me. . . . and then I wanted to push, and I pushed with everything in me. I've never strained so hard in all my life. And it was such a relief to do it. And I could feel the baby coming out. And then I yelled, this really wild animal yell . . . when I pushed the baby out, and it was perfect and I was nursing him on

> the delivery table, and I felt such triumph and so happy, I thought, "This is what Elizabeth wanted. This is how it should be."

Conclusion

> Sometimes when I feel dismay over the kinds of choices women seem to make about their births, I wonder why women are so incredibly passive. Why do we so often fail to reach out to other women after we have been through the experience of birth and learned so much about what does and does not work? Women who have themselves given birth know well what the price of docility can be . . . I say, why don't women ask for more? (Arms 1979: 79)

To a woman, my informants *did* ask for more. They did reach out--to the books, to the doctors, to their friends, to each other. The overwhelming irony is that in spite of all the books, the Lamaze classes, the involvement and complete participation of their husbands, all but two of them were to some extent victimized[15] --objectified, ignored, degraded, humiliated, and many were deeply and permanently wounded by their birth experiences. I have tried to show that some of the reasons lie in the deep beliefs of our society in the superiority of culture, especially technology, over nature, and in the certainly related socialization of women, to be 1) afraid of their bodies, especially their sexual and reproductive functions and 2) "good"--good girls, good students, good listeners, good in bed, good wives and mothers, *good patients.* It is because the pregnancy/birth/newborn period *is* a rite of passage, and precisely because the baby is born during the liminal--i.e., the most special, heightened, sensitive, delicate, and extremely *vulnerable* period in any rite of passage, that the stress and distress of the hospital experience can have such strong and lasting negative effects. The woman who goes into the hospital seeing herself as Earth Mother and comes out with a Cesarean scar is going to have difficulty reconciling those images.

So the childbirth narratives like Darla's, so full of pain under the surface of the humor with which they are often told, become serious attempts to integrate the traumas and humiliations of the birth experience into the concept of self that we normally hold. As such, they form an extension of the liminal phase of the rite of passage, an ongoing re-creative attempt to achieve some redemption of the loss that occurs when the doctor takes for himself the transformative increase in value that should attach to the woman (Davis-Floyd 1986b: 329-347).

This transformative power of rites of passage is recognized in many other cultures. Utilization of the perspective that anthropology provides--which can interpret pregnancy in this culture as an often-failed rite of passage, and can separate out the cultural tensions which lead to that failure[16] --may also point to the sources of that tension. Obviously they go very deep. Across the nation, it has taken the individual and group efforts of mothers, midwives, proponents of birthing techniques such as the Lamaze and Bradley methods, groups like La Leche League, C-Sec, NAPSAC (National Association of Parents and Professionals for Safe Alternatives in Childbirth), and other local and national coalitions of parents--as well as many concerned nurses and doctors--to bring about changes in the American way of birth. Among others, these changes include the mother's conscious participation in the delivery, fathers in the delivery room, birthing centers in hospitals, rooming-in of the newborn, a tremendous upsurge in breast-feeding (Parfitt 1980), and a recent dramatic increase in the number of midwife-attended and home births. In spite of these advances, the experiences of my informants and the findings of the other authors frequently cited in this paper indicate that the war is far from won. What these changes have done is to cause a tremendous increase in the number of women seeking satisfying "natural" pregnancies and childbirths; what they have not succeeded in doing is to sway the medical profession from its pathological definition of pregnancy/childbirth and its stubborn adherence to the more-intervention-the-better rule.

I feel that anthropology can be of great heuristic value in bridging this gulf between the mother and the medical profession, because I do not believe that doctors alone are responsible for our widespread cultural abdication of responsibility for our own bodies to the medical profession. This phenomenon, remarkable in a society where so much value is placed on freedom, choice, and self-control, stems from deep roots in this culture's underlying symbolic system.

Just about every society labels some of the human body's basic biological processes as polluting and dangerous, and proceeds to hedge them about with careful rituals and taboos. Why does this society pick on birth in particular to ritually isolate behind hospital walls? And why do we insist that people die in hospitals?[17] It seems to me that a comprehensive structural study of this culture's notions of pollution and danger will be necessary for an understanding of our cultural ambivalence towards our bodies and their natural processes. Once achieved, this understanding might do much toward uniting the interests of doctors, pregnant women, and American society that now seem radically opposed. If we want to improve our abysmal infant mortality rate,[18] and nurture the family as an institution,[19] we must recognize the cultural and individual importance of fulfilling rites of passage for crucial life-crisis events. We will have to try to arrive at a birthing process that can combine the advances of medical technology (where they are truly useful) with the universal need for shared transformative ritual.

Acknowledgement: My deepest thanks go to Beverly J. Stoeltje for her absolutely invaluable guidance, suggestions, and encouragement; and to Megan Biesele for creating my first opportunity to organize and present these ideas, and for her continuing help and support in carrying them through. Much gratitude also goes to Nancy Edwards, Claire R. Farrer, Christopher Crocker, Alma Gottlieb, and Jesse Green; and special thanks to Jo Ann Hassell for the typing and the talking, and to Cyndie and Robert for the time.

1. A cross-culturally common theme in creation myths treats the puzzle of two-or-many emerging from one. (My thanks to Beverly Stoeltje for helping me to see this connection.)

2. Mary Douglas (1966; 1972), Edmund Leach (1972) and others have demonstrated how many societies react with suspicion and fear to creatures and things which do not comfortably conform to the established categories in terms of which the society classifies and so gives order to the world. A classic example is the ambivalence with which many cultures regard body effluvia--feces, urine, mucus, saliva, tears, perspiration, semen, vaginal fluids, nail clippings, vomit, hair, blood--all of which cross our bodily boundaries and so pose difficult questions of what is me and not-me, human and not-human. Consequently, some or all of these substances are regarded as sacred or dangerous, and accorded special treatment in most--and perhaps all--cultures.

3. See Davis-Floyd 1986b for more detailed discussion of the three phases of the pregnancy/childbirth rite of passage in the U.S.

4. Richard Seel (1986), writing about childbirth in Great Britain, makes the relevant point that the lack of appropriate rituals of re-integration may be a major cultural cause of post-partum depression among new parents.

5. This process of social and subsequent self-symbolization has many ramifications and deserves further investigation.

6. The reality is that most American women actively choose the medicalization of their births to some degree, as this medicalization plays a major role in liberating them from the nineteenth century cultural view of motherhood as the central defining feature of women's lives.

7. Our medical profession is a microcosm of American society as a whole; its values and world view constitute a condensed version of the core value and belief system of the wider society. The actual purpose of the rituals of hospital birth (otherwise known as obstetrical procedures) is to socialize birthing women into the belief system of the dominant society. This socialization process is critical to the perpetuation of our society, as it is the mothers themselves who will then go on to socialize their children into our society's core value system, thus assuring its perpetuation (Davis-Floyd 1986b, 1986d).

8. Recent studies indicate that standing and walking during labor actually enlarges the woman's pelvis up to 1.5 centimeters more than it will expand if the woman remains supine. This extra enlargement will often be enough to make the difference between a successful vaginal delivery and a Cesarean section due to cephalopelvic disproportion. (This information comes to me via Sheila Richardson, R.N., ten-year Lamaze instructor, and member of ASPO [American Society for Psychoprophylaxis in Obstetrics] from a report made at the July, 1981 ASPO conference in Washington, D.C..)

9. I want to stress that I am speaking here only of the routine administering of the IV to normal obstetrical patients, and not to those conditions under which the IV is medically necessary to replace blood loss. These extremely rare conditions would include: placenta previa, in which the placenta implants under the fetus near or over the cervix--the frequency rate of this condition is around 0.4 percent (Pritchard and MacDonald 1980: 508); placental abruption--partial or complete separation of the placenta from the uterine wall, with a frequency rate of about 0.5 percent (496); rupture of the uterus, which varies in frequency among institutions from one in 100 to one in 11,000 (86); and the aforementioned post-partum hemorrhage. These

conditions can usually be either detected or predicted in advance and an IV duly administered. The latter three are often the avoidable results of medical intervention: among other things, all three can be brought on by too much pitocin (426, 791, 878), as can post-partum hypotension and shock (426). Moreover, *Williams Obstetrics* (497) indicates that the most common cause of placental abruption may be maternal hypertension (high blood pressure), which, as the Brewers (1977: 42-94) have shown, is itself often the result of malnutrition. See footnote 10.

I refer once again to the latest version of the widely used textbook, *Williams Obstetrics*:

> Although it has become customary in many hospitals to establish an intravenous infusion system routinely early in labor, there is seldom any real need for such in the normally pregnant woman at least until analgesia is administered. An intravenous infusion system is advantageous during the immediate puerperium [period immediately after birth] in order to administer oxytocin . . . when uterine hypotonicity [dysfunction] persists. Moreover, with longer labors, the administration of glucose, some salts, and water to the otherwise fasting woman at the rate of 60 to 120 ml. per hour is efficacious (Pritchard and MacDonald 1980: 414).

This rule, that "in essentially all circumstances, food and oral fluids should be withheld during active labor and delivery" *(Ibid.)* is followed in many hospitals, and often itself necessitates the use of the IV to prevent the dehydration which can result in maternal hypotension (low blood pressure) and shock.

10. Now that X-rays of the fetus have been proven to cause cancer in the developing child, doctors are taught to routinely recommend ultrasound exams instead. The mother's faith and trust in the miracles of science are reinforced when she sees the outline of her baby on the screen. The exam is now being used on more than a million women a year (Mendelsohn 1981: 164). The risks it may carry are rarely

mentioned. Mendelsohn has this to say:

> External monitors, which use ultrasound to penetrate the mother's body and produce sound waves that measure the condition of the fetus, may pose risks that have yet to be revealed . . . Researchers at the FDA Bureau of Radiological Health, noting independent studies revealing harmful effects from ultrasound, said more study is needed before the safety of the procedure can be determined. In 1973, a study revealed changes in amniotic fluid that had been exposed to ultrasound. Of 65 amniotic fluid specimens taken from patients who had been exposed to ultrasound, 35 (60 percent) failed to grow on culture media. Only 13 of 106 specimens (12 percent) obtained from patients who had not been exposed failed to grow. Investigators also have found delayed neurological development, altered emotional and behavioral effects, fetal abnormalities, and blood and vascular changes in animals exposed to ultrasound (Mendelsohn 1981: 164).

This evidence is inconclusive: the point is that this ultrasound exam, or sonogram, is well on its way to being prescribed for all pregnancies, just as X-rays were routine some years ago.

11. Toxemia is a potentially fatal condition of late pregnancy, manifested in maternal high blood pressure (hypertension), edema (swelling), protein in the urine and weight gain of "more than 3 pounds per week" (Wynn 1979: 99, 101). Gail and Tom Brewer (1977) present a well-documented and convincing argument that malnutrition is the chief cause of toxemia, and that well-nourished pregnant women who are diagnosed as toxemic are usually misdiagnosed, simply because they exhibit normal signs of pregnancy, such as water retention and swelling of the face, hands, arms, or legs (edema). The Brewers insist that calories and salt are essential ingredients for normal placental function during pregnancy; thus doctors who commonly prescribe low-calorie, no-sodium diets for the pregnant women they

misdiagnose as toxemic, in so doing are actually causing the women to develop toxemia (pre-eclampsia). If the toxemic (pre-eclampsic) condition is aggravated by continued restriction of sodium and calories, convulsions (eclampsia) may well result, and/or fetal death. Consequently, symptoms of "toxemia" are a frequent cause for labor induction and Cesarean section (Pritchard and MacDonald 1980; Wynn 1979). In spite of the Brewers' findings, *Williams Obstetrics* (Pritchard and MacDonald 1980: 666) states: "The cause or causes of pre-eclampsia, eclampsia, and essential hypertension remain for the most part unknown, despite decades of intensive research . . ."--a phenomenon which seems to go hand-in-hand with the lack of courses on nutrition in medical school.

12. See Davis-Floyd 1986b: 348-365 for a discussion of medical school as a rite of passage in which those becoming doctors are thoroughly socialized into the core value system of American society, so that they, as society's representatives, in turn may socialize us.

13. The reader will note that a number of books and articles which oppose medical intervention in normal childbirth are written by M.D.'s. Alternative childbirth organizations such as ASPO, NAPSAC (National Association of Parents and Professionals for Safe Alternatives in Childbirth), and others list many obstetrician/gynecologists as participating members, although these comprise but a small percentage of obstetrician/gynecologists in the United States.

    Medical textbooks themselves are beginning to incorporate some non-interventionist ideas. For example, Niswander (1976: 423) includes a brief statement on the importance of bonding (see footnote 19); and the newest *Williams Obstetrics* opposes rupture of the membranes during labor (Pritchard and MacDonald 1980: 414), includes one report on the benefits of walking during labor (413), and flatly states: "A common tendency, especially at large, busy public institutions, has been too little 'laying on of hands' to gauge the quality of labor, and too much 'putting in of hands' to identify cervical dilatation" (413).

14. My thanks to Nancy Edwards for pointing this out.

15. Recent feminist scholarship (Dubois et al. 1985) has urged us to look beyond the concept of the woman as a passive victim, as this concept limits our ability to understand the degree to which many of us have become active agents in our own socialization processes. See Davis-Floyd 1986b: 210-328 for an in-depth exploration of the reasons why the majority of American women actively *choose* the medicalization of their births.

16. Can rites of passage be said to "fail" or "succeed"? If their object is individual enhancement and personal growth, then, from the point of view of most of the women in my study group, hospital birth rituals can be said to have failed. But if their object is socialization, then from the point of view of the wider society, the question for investigation then becomes: to what degree have these birth rituals succeeded in their didactic and socializing purposes, and to what extent does that success manifest itself in these women's daily lives?

17. "We note, first of all, that in the United States birth is overwhelmingly seen as a medical event. This is consistent with the fact that in contemporary U.S. society, physiological processes in general fall into the medical domain. Thus, nutrition, sexual adjustment, sleeping patterns, mood swings, obesity, learning difficulties, alcoholism, drug use, violence, dying, and all sorts of 'deviance' are considered proper subjects for medical attention" (Jordan 1980: 35).

18. The rate of infant mortality in the U.S. continues to be one of the worst among developed countries in the world today; we rank fourteenth (Parfitt 1980: 169).

19. Many recent studies indicate that the birthing process is much more significant for future family relationships than previously realized. Parents who were not allowed to bond with their children for a long period of time following birth have a statistically greater chance of becoming child abusers in the future (Parfitt 1980: 150). Both fathers and mothers who participate in the birth and are able to

bond with the child immediately following it, show closer relationships with those children, and express more satisfaction with the parent-child relationship one year after the birth than do those who are not. Peterson-Mehl (1977), Feldman (1978), Arms (1979), Parfitt (1980), and Pearce (1980) provide more informative summaries of recent bonding studies. Parfitt reports: ". . . the period immediately following an uncomplicated birth is a time of quiet alertness and emotional euphoria for parents who are allowed to be together with their new baby. At this time occurs . . . the establishment of powerful attachments between mother and baby, father and baby, and between mother and father . . . Bonding is essentially accomplished by sight, touch, and smell. Eye-to-eye contact and skin-to-skin contact are all-important" (1980: 33).

References Cited

Arms, Suzanne
1977 Why Women Must Be in Control of Childbirth and Feminine Health Services, *in* Stewart and Stewart (below).

1979 (1975) Immaculate Deception. New York: Bantam Books.

Benson, Ralph C., M.D.
1980 Handbook of Obstetrics and Gynecology. Seventh Edition. Los Altos, California: Lange Medical Publications.

Beuf, Ann Hill
1979 Biting Off the Bracelet: A Study of Children in Hospitals. Philadelphia: University of Pennsylvania Press.

Birnbaum, David
1977 The Iatrogenesis of Damaged Mothers and Babies at Birth. *In* Stewart and Stewart (below).

Brackbill, Yvonne, J. Rice, and Diony Young
1984 Birth Trap: The Legal Low-Down on High-Tech Obstetrics. St. Louis: C. V. Mosby.

Brewer, Gail Sforza and Tom Brewer, M.D.
1977 What Every Pregnant Woman Should Know: The Truth about Diet and Drugs in Pregnancy. New York: Penguin Books.

Cafferata, John, ed.
1975 Rites. New York: McGraw-Hill.

Crocker, Jon Christopher
1985 Vital Souls. University of Arizona Press.

Davis-Floyd, Robbie E.
1986a Afterword: The Cultural Context of Changing Childbirth. *In* The Healing Power of Birth, Rima Beth Star, ed. Austin, Texas: Star Publishing.

1986b Birth as an American Rite of Passage. Ph.D. dissertation, Dept. of Anthropology/Folklore,

University of Texas at Austin. Ann Arbor, Michigan: University Microfilms. Publication No. 86-18448.

1986c Routines and Rituals: A New View. NAACOG (Nurses Association of the American College of Obstetrics and Gynecology), Update Series, Princeton Continuing Professional Education Center.

1986d Birth as an American Rite of Passage. *In* The Anthropology of Childbirth in America, Karen Michaelson, ed. Hadley, Maryland: Bergin and Garvey.

Derber, Anton
1979 The Pursuit of Attention: Power and Individualism in Everyday Life. Cambridge, Mass.: Schenkman.

Douglas, Mary
1966 Purity and Danger. London: Routledge and Kegan Paul.

1972 Pollution. *In* Reader in Comparative Religion, William A. Lessa and Evon Z. Vogt, eds. Third Edition. New York: Harper and Row.

Dubois, Ellen C., Gail P. Kelly, Elizabeth L. Kennedy, Carolyn W. Korsmeyer and Lillian S. Robinson
1985 Feminist Scholarship: Kindling in the Groves of Academe. Urbana and Chicago: University of Illinois Press.

Dundes, Alan
1980 Interpreting Folklore. Bloomington: Indiana University Press.

Ehrenreich, Barbara, and Deirdre English
1973 Witches, Midwives and Nurses: A History of Woman Healers. Old Westbury, N.Y.: The Feminist Press.

Eliade, Mircea
1975 Modern Man's Need to Understand the Rites of Passage. *In* Cafferta 1975 (above).

Ettner, Frederic, M.D.
1977 Hospital Obstetrics: Do the Benefits Outweigh the Risks? *In* Stewart and Stewart (below).

Feldman, Dr. Sylvia
1978 Choices in Childbirth. New York: Grosset and Dunlap.

Goffman, Erving
1961 Asylums. New York: Anchor Books.

Graebner, Alan
1975 Growing Up Female. *In* The Nacirema. James R. Spradley and Michael Rynkiewich, eds. Boston: Little, Brown.

Haire, Doris
1972 The Cultural Warping of Childbirth, International Childbirth Education Association News. Milwaukee, Wisconsin.

Harrison, Michelle, M.D.
1977 Birth as the First Experiencing of Motherhood. *In* Stewart and Stewart (below).

Hazell, Lester Dessez
1976 (1969) Commonsense Childbirth. New York: Berkeley Medallion Books.

Inch, Sally
1984 Birth Rights: What Every Parent Should Know about Childbirth in Hospitals. New York: Pantheon Books.

Jordan, Brigitte
1980 Birth in Four Cultures. Montreal: Eden (orig. pub. 1978).

Kalčik, Susan
1975 '. . . like Ann's gynecologist or the time I was almost raped': Personal Narratives in Women's Rap Groups, *In* Women and Folklore, Clair R. Farrer, ed. Austin: University of Texas Press.

Kiester, Edwin, Jr., and Sally Valente Kiester
1981 The Better Homes and Gardens New Baby Book. New York: Bantam Books.

Kitzinger, Sheila
1970 Women as Mothers. New York: Vintage Books.

Labov, William, and Joshua Waletzky
1966 Narrative Analysis: Oral Versions of Personal Experience, American Ethnological Society Proceedings, pp. 12-44.

Lakoff, George and Mark Johnson
1980 Metaphors We Live By. Chicago: University of Chicago Press.

Leach, Edmund
1972 "Animal Categories and Verbal Abuse." *In* Reader in Comparative Religion, William A. Lessa and Evon Z. Vogt, eds. Third edition. New York: Harper and Row.

LeBaron, Charles
1981 Gentle Vengeance: An Account of the First Year at Harvard Medical School. New York: Richard Marek.

Lee, Dorothy
1950 Codifications of Reality: Lineal and Nonlineal. Psycho-Somatic Medicine 12: 89-97.

Levy, Barry S., Frederick S. Wilkinson, and William M. Marine
1971 Reducing Neonatal Mortality Rate with Nurse-Midwives. American Journal of Obstetrics and Gynecology 109: 50-58.

Mehl, Lewis E., M.D.
1977 Scientific Research on Childbirth Alternatives: What Can It Tell Us ABout Hospital Practice? *In* Stewart and Stewart (below).

Mendelsohn, Robert, M.D.
1979 Confessions of a Medical Heretic. Chicago: Contemporary Books.

1981 Mal(e) Practice: How Doctors Manipulate Women. Chicago: Contemporary Books.

Newton, Niles
1977 Effects of Fear and Disturbances on Labor. *In* Stewart and Stewart (below).

Niswander, Kenneth, M.D.
1976 Obstetrics: Essentials of Clinical Practice. Boston: Little, Brown.

Ortner, Sherry
1974 Is Female to Male as Nature Is to Culture? *In* Woman, Culture and Society, Michelle Zimbalist Rosaldo and Louise Lamphere, eds. Stanford: Stanford University Press.

Parfitt, Rebecca Rowe
1980 The Birth Primer: A Source Book of Traditional and Alternative Methods in Labor and Delivery. New York: Signet Books.

Pearce, Joseph Chilton
1980 Magical Child. New York: Bantam Books.

Peterson, Gail H., M.S.S.W., and Lewis E. Mehl, M.D.
1977 Studies of Psychological Outcome for Various Childbirth Alternatives. *In* Stewart and Stewart (below).

Pritchard, Jack A., M.D., and Paul C. MacDonald, M.D.
1980 Williams Obstetrics, 16th Edition. New York: Appleton-Century-Crofts.

Rich, Adrienne
1977 Of Woman Born: Motherhood as Experience and Institution. New York: Bantam Books.

Ridington, Robin
1979 The Hunting and Gathering World View in Relation to Adaptive Strategy. Manuscript.

Rothman, Barbara Katz
1986 Tentative Pregnancy: Prenatal Diagnosis and the Future of Motherhood. New York: Viking.

Seel, Richard M.
1986a Birth Rate. Health Visitor, 59: (6): 182-184.

1986b The Making of the Modern Father. Bath, England: Gateway Books.

Star, Rima Beth
1984 The Healing Power of Birth. Austin, Texas: Star Publishing.

Stein, Leonard
1967 The Doctor-Nurse Game. Archives of General Psychiatry 16: 699-703.

Stewart, Lee and David Stewart, eds.
1976 Safe Alternatives in Childbirth. Marble Hill, Missouri: NAPSAC (National Association of Parents and Professionals for Safe Alternatives in Childbirth).

1977 Twenty-first Century Obstetrics Now! Vols. 1, 2. Marble Hill, Missouri: NAPSAC.

1979 Compulsory Hospitalization, or Freedom of Choice in Childbirth? Vols. 1, 2, 3. Marble Hill, Missouri: NAPSAC.

1981 The Five Standards for Safe Childbearing. Marble Hill, Missouri: NAPSAC.

Sutton-Smith, Brian
1972 Games of Order and Disorder. Paper presented to Symposium: Forms of Symbolic Inversion. American Anthropological Association, Toronto.

Tucker, Tarvez with Elisabeth Bing
1975 Prepared Childbirth. Wayne, Pennsylvania: Banbury Books.

Turner, Victor W.
1968 The Drums of Affliction: A Study of Religious Processes among the Ndembu of Zambia. London: Oxford University Press.

1969 The Ritual Process: Structure and Anti-Structure. Chicago: Aldine.

1964 Betwixt and Between: The Liminal Period in *Rites de Passage. In* Proceedings of the American Ethnological Society Symposium on New Approaches to the Study of Religion. Seattle: University of Washington Press.

1974 Liminal to Liminoid in Play, Flow, and Ritual: An Essay in Comparative Symbology. Rice University Studies, 60 (3): 53-92.

Van Gennep, Arnold
1966 (1908) The Rites of Passage. Chicago: University of Chicago Press.

Warner, W. Lloyd
1959 The Living and the Dead: A Study of the Symbolic Life of Americans. New Haven, Connecticut: Yale University Press.

Wynn, Ralph M.
1979 Obstetrics and Gynecology: The Clinical Core. Philadelphia: Lea and Febiger.

Cross-Cultural Perspectives on Middle-Aged Women[1]

Judith K. Brown

> At a certain age the men writers change into old Mother Hubbard. The women writers become Joan of Arc without the fighting.
>
> --Ernest Hemingway, *The Green Hills of Africa*

Middle-aged women have been largely overlooked in the cross-cultural study of human development, supposedly for lack of appropriate ethnographic data. Indeed, studies which focus on middle-aged women are rare (but see Kerns 1980a), and much fieldwork has been informed by a pro-youth, pro-male bias (Griffen 1977). Yet there are many ethnographies which provide revealing glimpses of older women dispensing the household food, arranging marriages, or preparing for a ceremony. What frequently remains unreported is the relationship between a mother and her adult offspring, probably because the enduring nature of this bond is not strongly emphasized in our own society.

The real difficulties in the study of middle-aged women are the lack of demographic data and the problem of definition. When are women middle-aged? Do women constitute a recognized category, and one large enough to merit examination? I assume that the answer to the latter question is yes, and I define middle-aged women as mothers who are not yet aged but who have adult offspring. I am avoiding the term "menopausal" because I want to convey a social rather than a physiological meaning and because I am referring to a longer period in women's lives than the time of actual physical change. Therefore, I will omit consideration of the growing body of cross-cultural studies of menopause and menopausal symptoms,[2] as well as studies of widowhood, witches, and the aged.

My purpose is to examine the discontinuity in women's lives as they age beyond the childbearing years. I will begin with descriptive data drawn largely from the works of Bart (1969), Griffen (1977), Kaufert (1979), and Kerns (1979, 1980) and from my own previous exploration of the literature (Brown 1979). Although the examples are from simple and complex societies in many different settings and practicing varied subsistence activities, there is amazing unanimity in the findings. Women's lives appear to improve with the onset of middle age. In some societies this change is dramatic and in others moderate. I will consider the interpretations of these findings suggested by psychoanalytic theory, sociobiology, and the work of Gutmann, Goody, and the Whitings, and I will offer another interpretation that stresses the relationship of middle-aged women with their adult children.

Positive Changes in Women's Positions

Bart (1969) and Kaufert (1979) have reported evidence of lowered status for women after the childbearing years in a few societies, and Davis (1979) has suggested that the position of women in a Newfoundland fishing community remains unchanged by menopause. These are the exceptions. The "forty-year-old jitters," the "empty nest syndrome," and the "rolelessness" which have been ascribed to middle-aged women in Western society (see Henry 1977, Bart 1970, Skultans 1970)[3] simply do not apply cross-culturally. Overwhelmingly, the cross-cultural evidence indicates positive changes. Middle age brings fewer restrictions, the right to exert authority over certain kinsmen, and the opportunity for achievement and recognition beyond the household.

Removal of Restrictions

Whether there is a reduction in the restrictions on women or the addition of new privileges, all the researchers note some of the following changes: First, menstrual customs no longer apply, since women can no longer cause contamination and disaster in those societies harboring such beliefs concerning menstruation. Second, once their sexuality can have no consequences, women are often regarded as asexual. Beyond childbearing, a woman can no longer bring dishonor upon her family by sexual adventuring, real or imputed. No longer need her alleged sexual voracity (Dwyer 1978)[4] and capacity for making mischief be curbed. Women are freed from male authority and from the need to exhibit deferential behavior. For example, in the Moslem Kelantan Malay village described by Raybeck (1979), public deference toward the husband is required of young women, as well as modesty in dress and action. A young woman is not permitted to frequent the village coffee shops, yet an older woman actually runs one of these. According to Raybeck, the freedom of middle age is also enjoyed by divorced women, and hence divorce is viewed (in part) as premature access to the privileges of the postchildbearing years. In many societies various improprieties are overlooked in older women: older women may urinate in public, violate food and language taboos (Mead 1949, Griffen 1977), or even drink too much on ceremonial occasions (Kerns 1979). However, changes in norms and behavior are reported not only for societies in which women are believed to be polluting or in need of restraint, but also for societies with a more egalitarian ideology. Thus even among the !Kung, trance behavior (a masculine prerogative) is not exhibited by younger women, but older women do occasionally go into trance (Marshall and Biesele 1974).

In some societies, as among the Black Carib of Belize, younger women may restrict their movements, fearing gossip about their sexual conduct (Kerns 1979). In some societies, customs such as purdah entirely confine some young women to the home. Even in the absence of such constraints, the geographic mobility of most young women is curtailed by the demands of child care, by subsistence activities, and by household responsibilities. Only as a woman ages is a greater variety of settings made available. For example, Marshall (1964) reports that Yoruba women's marketing activities are closely related to the demands of child care. As these diminish, a woman is freed for profitable long-distance trade activities (also see Raybeck 1979). Roy (1975) reports that older, upper-class urban Bengali women can leave the confines of purdah in order to make one or two annual religious pilgrimages, the expense of which is noted by neighbors and augments family prestige. Even the Yanomamö, whose ethnography prompted formulation of the "male supremacist complex" (Divale and Harris 1976),[5] allow mobility to older women. Chagnon (1968) reports that older women enjoy a unique neutrality during the endemic intervillage warfare and travel to enemy villages to retrieve the bodies of the slain. In distinct contrast to the harsh treatment accorded younger women by their husbands, older women are treated kindly by their adult children. In a more recent account, Ramos (1979) reports that women are not helpless pawns in the political machinations of their male kinsmen as Chagnon has suggested. Women are consulted and exercise decision-making power. Although Ramos does not specify the ages of the women she describes, some of her examples are women with adult children. There is not necessarily a contradiction in the Yanomamö data: the position of women changes with age.

Authority Over Kin

A second major area of change is that older women are expected to exert authority over specified kinsmen. They have the right to extract labor from them and/or to exercise decision-making power over them. These rights are not the result of coincidence or of a forceful personality, but are socially recognized and institutionalized. Apoko (1967) reports that among the Acholi the mother of a grown and marriageable daughter enjoys considerable leisure and the opportunity to visit with friends. Her daughter attends to the household chores. To attract suitors, a marriageable girl makes sure that her home looks well cared for and is generously supplied with firewood. Since the marriage of his sister provides the cattle that will enable a young man to marry, he takes an interest in the housekeeping skills of his unmarried sister and the visible leisure of his mother. Among the Iroquois, on the other hand, it was the son-in-law who was expected to please his mother-in-law by providing meat for the family of his bride. If his mother-in-law was not satisfied with his efforts, she could terminate his marriage and banish him from the matrilocal longhouse (see Brown 1970).

In addition to the right to command the labor of certain designated members of the younger generation, older women frequently exercise power over important decisions affecting the lives of their juniors. Hayes (1975) and Janice Boddy (personal communication 1981) attribute the perpetuation of the practice of infibulation in the Sudan to the powerful influence of older women. Even though long outlawed, this excruciatingly painful and dangerous genital mutilation is practiced on all little girls and on mothers after the birth of each child. Older women insist that the operation is necessary to insure the moral character of women and the honor of the lineage.

In a number of societies decisions about marriage, often attributed to men by male ethnographers, are in actuality very much under the influence of older women. Hamilton (1970) reports on the role of older women in the important process of wife bestowal among the Australian Aborigines, whose practice of polygyny creates a chronic shortage of women available for marriage (also see Bell 1980). According to Lee (1981), older !Kung women are experts on kin terms and thus charged with classifying people; these classifications, in turn, are the basis for arranging marriages. Among the Kafe of New Guinea, according to Faithorn (1976), the mother of the wife-to-be, the adoptive mother or mothers of the wife-to-be, the mother of the groom, and the wives of the groom's father's brothers (and sometimes his adult sisters and the sisters of his father) all have crucial roles to play in the many decisions involved in each marriage negotiation within the tribe. Of Moroccan Muslim society, which confines and restricts women, Mernissi (1975) observes that sex segregation gives the mother of the groom-to-be access to crucial information regarding a potential wife. Only she can actually see the girl, talk to her, and gather information about her physical attributes from the attendants at the local bath:

> The power of the elderly woman as both the receiver and broadcaster of information concerning young women gives her tremendous power in deciding who is going to marry whom and reduces the man's decision-making role significantly. (Mernissi 1975: 71)

In a society like that described by Mernissi, which separates male and female worlds, women beyond child-bearing provide the link between the two. Their role of go-between gives them a position of power and importance.

On the other hand, Bart (1969) has suggested that institutionalization of the mother-in-law and/or the grandmother role tends to be associated with higher status for middle-aged women. According to Bart, patrilocality, extended-family residence, and stress on allegiance to the family of orientation (as opposed to strong marital ties) all serve to consolidate the mother-in-law role. Indeed, the behavior and position of women change dramatically in those societies in which the young girl moves into the household of her husband and his family at marriage. At first she is in a position of servitude, separated from her own kinsmen, living under the authority of her mother-in-law, and treated as an outsider even by her husband. It is the birth of sons that raises her status. As these sons mature, she becomes the imposing and respected mother-in-law, with authority over her daughters-in-law and the power to exert strong influence upon and through her grown sons. The latter are often more deeply attached to her than to their young wives.

A full description of this metamorphosis is provided by Roy (1975: 126) whose report is based upon the detailed life histories of some fifty upper-class Bengali women. The young bride, homesick for her village and family, restricted to life in purdah among strangers, compelled to demonstrate her industriousness and her respect for her husband's kinsmen, eventually becomes

> the *ginni-ma,* the matron-mother, a status that indicates the climax of a woman's life. Now she is important in her own standing . . . She has served and obeyed the elders; it's now her turn to be listened to and respected by all, including the men in the house. . . . She is no longer a woman who can be looked at with desire or pity, but she must be respected. The keys that open and lock several rooms including the kitchen, the pantry, and the storeroom symbolize her command and authority in the household--something her mother-in-law and older sister-in-law once enjoyed. (Roy 1975: 126).

Mernissi (1975) gives a strikingly similar account for traditional Moroccan Muslim society. Living in the household of her husband's family, the young bride is tutored and protected by her mother-in-law, for whom she performs daily prescribed deference rituals. When she becomes a mother-in-law, the submission of her daughters-in-law is required by modern law. The marriage of her sons strengthens her claim on their gratitude and love. The symbol of her domestic power is the key to the storage room where food is kept, and it is the mother-in-law who decides what is eaten by the household members and when.

This dramatic change from bride to mother-in-law in patrilocal societies is widely reported. Michaelson and Goldschmidt (1971: 339), on the basis of data from 46 peasant societies, conclude:

> In the patricentric household a woman's status and emotional ties both center on her relation

> to her sons . . . A woman's only official power role is that of mother-in-law, in which she exerts control over her sons' wives.

In the traditional Chinese family, according to Yang (1959), the grown son is his mother's "ally" (also see Wolf 1974). Srinivas (1977: 230) observes for India that

> as a young wife matured into a mother and mother-in-law, the relationship between the husband and wife became increasingly egalitarian. In fact, if anything, the balance was tilted in favor of the wife.

Hayes (1975: 624) provides similar observations for the Sudan:

> The older women achieve a status more closely resembling that of men. They have influence and authority over the daughters-in-law of the compound, as well as their own daughters still living at home. Mothers are greatly respected by their sons, and sons often have closer emotional ties to their mothers than to their stern patriarchal fathers. Grandmothers are as respected as fathers. (1963: 209)

Albert (1963: 209) reports for Burundi that

> When a woman is at last a mother-in-law and grandmother, she has reached the high point of her life as a woman.

She has the power to persuade her son to send a wife away, or she may overwork or even poison a daughter-in-law she does not like. Morsy (1978) reports that in rural Egypt an elderly household head may relinquish to his wife authority over the division of labor and the distribution of resources within the extended family household.

This vesting of authority in older women is not confined to patrilocal societies, although there the contrast with younger women's powerlessness is particularly dramatic. Authority for older women is also reported for matrilocal societies. Among the Mundurucú (Murphy and Murphy 1974), the oldest woman was in charge of the household, which sometimes contained more than fifty people. She administered the tedious and complicated food processing, which required the coordinated labor of many women, and she gave advice and acted as midwife. Her authority was undisputed but exercised with tact. Richards (1956) reports for the Bemba that the "shy and submissive" girl eventually becomes the "imperious and managing" older Bemba woman, who sits on the verandah of her hut, directing the activities of her younger kinsmen and supervising the distribution of food.

Achievement and Recognition

Third, as women age beyond the childbearing years, they are provided with new opportunities for achievement and for recognition beyond the household. A woman can become a midwife (see, for example, Hayes 1975, Paul and Paul 1975),[6] a holy woman (Kolenda 1978, Hungry Wolf 1980), a matchmaker (Wolf 1974), a medicine woman (Wright 1979a), a curer (Spring 1978), or a mistress of ceremonies at initiation rites (Richards 1956). Kerns (1979), Griffen (1977), and Bart (1969) report on the expanded religious and ceremonial activities of older women in a number of societies. In traditional times, matrons could aspire to religious office among the Iroquois (Brown 1970); they were able to influence the political life of the tribe and to exercise authority within the longhouse. Kehoe (1976) and Lewis (1941) report on the phenomenon of the manly-hearted woman among the Blackfoot. These were not masculine women, but women who were passionately sexual and favorite wives. Only older and wealthy women could aspire to manly-heartedness; in a younger woman such behavior would have been received with disdain. Blackfoot women could also aspire to be doctors, members of a women's society, and wives of medicine-bundle owners, but it was the Sun Dance which provided public recognition of Old Ladies--a term of respect (Kehoe 1976, Hungry Wolf 1980). Similarly, among the Bemba a number of special positions were reserved for older women. The *nacimbusa*, mistress of ceremonies at initiation rites, also acted as midwife for girls whose ceremonies she had directed (Richards 1956). Senior Bemba princesses ruled districts of their own. The sacred fire of the Bemba chief was watched by a senior wife past child-bearing, and the chief's shrines were guarded by certain old women. Other societies provide fewer opportunities for public recognition. Hayes (1975) reports that in the Sudan the only such position is that of midwife.

Theoretical Interpretations

These cross-cultural findings do not fit neatly into any theoretical framework, for a variety of reasons. First, theories of human development which apply to adulthood are few and incomplete. Erikson's (1950) "Eight Ages of Man" theory suggests the direction such a theory might take but has little applicability to women and takes no account of cross-cultural data. The work of Lowenthal, Thurnher and Chiriboga (1975) does stress sex differences in adulthood, but the analysis is based on an American sample and is culture-specific. A second difficulty with the data is that they raise not one but two basic questions: Why are the changes that come with middle age more dramatic in some societies than in others? How can these changes be accounted for in all societies? One explanation deals with variables, the other with constants.

Differences in Magnitude

As Bart (1969) has noted, the end of the childbearing years creates changes of varying magnitude: dramatic in some societies, less so in others. Two hypotheses may account for these differences. While they are not concerned with aspects of aging nor with the anthropology of women, they are surprisingly opposite.

Aspects of inheritance. Goody (1976) views systems of inheritance as the crucial link between the material/economic aspects of culture and social structure. It is through inheritance that property moves among kinsmen; hence its analysis requires knowledge of the forms that property takes as well as the relationships established by kinship. There are three broad categories in the analysis of inheritance. First, there may be no rules of transmission and no individual property rights, as was typical among traditional societies of North and South America. Second, there is "lateral" or "horizontal" inheritance, typical of most traditional African societies. This form of inheritance is associated with hoe cultivation and the absence of complex forms of stratification. Preference is given to brothers over sons in the inheritance of property. Males inherit from males and females from females. Third, there is "lineal" or "vertical" inheritance, typical of societies practicing intensive agriculture widespread in the Eurasian and Circum-Mediterranean culture areas. This type of inheritance functions to preserve the status of offspring in complex, stratified societies and is frequently associated with what Goody has called "divergent devolution," the non-sex-linked transfer of property. Women can inherit as well as men and may receive a premortem inheritance in the form of a dowry at marriage. In societies that practice divergent devolution, kinsmen exert strong control over the behavior of the young marriageable woman. The property and prestige of the family must not be placed in jeopardy by her sexual adventuring or by her marriage to a man of inferior station. Courtship is controlled by means of chaperones, the employment of go-betweens, and arranged marriages. Cousin marriage (such as to a father's brother's son) serves to keep the property within the extended family. There is concern over the sexuality of women and an emphasis upon virginity at marriage, for virginity insures that there will be no conflicting claims on the woman's estate. Goody asserts that where women are most propertied, they are also most restricted, particularly in matters pertaining to marriage.

Goody's analysis suggests that, once age has transformed her into someone to be inherited from, the woman who was supervised and restricted when young will experience a dramatic role change. Restrictions on an older woman's sexuality become unnecessary, since she will bear no more children. Restrictions on her mobility can be lifted. No longer supervised, *she* supervises her daughters-in-law and her unmarried daughters. She exerts power through and with the support of her grown sons and may even dominate an aged husband. In societies which practice other types of inheritance, women might be expected to be less supervised and restricted and hence to experience a less dramatic change at the end of the child-bearing years.

Relations between Spouses. A second theoretical approach to this variation in magnitude is suggested by Whiting and Whiting's (1975) cross-cultural study of aloofness and intimacy between husbands and wives. In societies at a certain stage of cultural complexity, there is property to be protected (such as cattle) but insufficient specialization to provide an army or police force. Such societies depend upon a cadre of warriors. The pugnacity and valor which characterize a good warrior are promoted by the separation of the sexes in daily life: spouses do not eat together, sleep together, or relax together, nor do they share in child-rearing chores. Such patterns of aloofness may be reinforced by beliefs in female impurity and contamination.

This implies that when women reach middle age and men are too old to be warriors, the separation of the sexes can be relaxed. Beliefs in female impurity no longer pertain. Indeed, the older woman past menstruation and child rearing can be a liaison between the separate worlds of men and women. Most societies do not call for aloofness between spouses, and therefore the changes which come with middle age in these societies are less dramatic.

The hypotheses suggested by the work of Goody and by that of the Whitings complement rather than contradict each other. Goody's work singles out complex societies in the Eurasian and Circum-Mediterranean culture areas, whereas Whiting and Whiting identify certain less complex societies with a worldwide distribution. Women in both types of societies would be predicted to experience a more dramatic discontinuity between the childbearing and post-childbearing years. Once ratings are developed, a cross-cultural test of these hypotheses will be possible.

Discontinuity: Explaining the Constant

The second major question raised by the cross-cultural findings seeks an explanation for the discontinuity in women's lives. Why does middle age bring fewer restrictions, increased authority over kinsmen, and greater opportunity for achievement and recognition? Since the changes appear to be virtually universal, the panhuman physiological aspects of middle age--the end of fertility and menstruation--provide a partial explanation, at least for the easing of certain restrictions, but additional explanations are needed.

Personality development. Traditional psychoanalytic theory[7] tends to emphasize early life experiences, and a male viewpoint predominates. Deutsch's (1945) work on the psychology of women does, however, contain an epilogue on the climacterium, which she considers the "partial death" of women once they cease to be "servants of the species." She sees the physiological changes of menopause as harbingers of death and stresses the cyclical nature of women's lives, noting the similarities between puberty and climacterium. As the father was the forbidden sex object early in life, so is the mature son for the aging mother, and yet an intense bond develops. For Deutsch, the climacterium is a time for fantasy gratification, "for reality has actually become poor in prospects, and resignation without compensation is often the only solution" (Deutsch 1945: 477). Deutsch's gloomy view is not, however, supported by the cross-cultural evidence, and neither is her emphasis on the cyclical nature of women's lives. Although initiation rites for girls at puberty were once practiced by many societies, none have been reported for the celebration of menopause. The economic role of women is related to the practice of female initiation rites (Brown 1963, 1978), but there appears to be no relationship between economic roles and the position of menopausal women (Barth 1969). On the other hand, Deutsch's emphasis on the relationship between a mature son and his mother does receive some cross-cultural support, as suggested by Mernissi (1975), Roy (1975), and others above.

A more positive psychoanalytic view is provided by Benedek (1950), who refers to the climacteric as a "developmental phase." She suggests that "the desexualization of the emotional needs . . . releases psychic energies for sublimation and further integration of the personality" (Benedek 1950: 26). This view can also be inferred from a recent paper by Beatrice Whiting (1980). Although concerned with child rearing and not with middle-aged women, Whiting's formulations are relevant to the increased geographic mobility which older women in many societies experience. Whiting's data indicate that it is assignment of the settings in which "mundane social behavior" is played out that has the most potent effect in the socialization of children. Each setting brings with it actors of certain ages and of a certain sex, appropriate activities, and norms which govern behavior. A child learns habits of interpersonal behavior because of assigned settings. As a person ages, new settings require different behaviors and also require learning about activities, actors, and norms not previously encountered. Women whose movement has been restricted during the childbearing years and who are given geographic mobility later in life enjoy tremendous opportunities for learning at that time. Like Benedek's, Whiting's formulations suggest a new developmental phase rather than forebodings of death and retreat into fantasy.

Parental investment and reproductive success. A totally different interpretation is suggested by sociobiology, which creates an imaginative projection into the remote human past. Here is a vision of man, the eternal philanderer, and woman, the hapless drudge immersed in child care, each striving to project his or her own unique genetic endowment into eternity. To its detractors, sociobiology is a mere fantasy (a male fantasy), first because its postulates as stated are not amenable to proof or disproof (see Shapiro 1980) and second because heritability is posited for propensities and behaviors which are widely regarded as cultural and learned.

For sociobiology, survival beyond the childbearing years presents something of an anomaly, and its purpose in the scheme of things is difficult to explain. Campbell (1966: 270) suggests two possible reasons a "postreproductive period of life can be of value to evolving man." First, since children mature slowly, a postreproductive period is essential for the survival of the lastborn child. Second, since humans depend upon learned behavior, the older individual provides wisdom and information. In the case of older women, such knowledge would be related in part to childbirth, child rearing, and the household arts (also see Barash 1977).

Dawkins (1976) considers menopause an "adaptation" to the survival by women to ages at which a grandchild born at the same time as a child has a better chance of survival. Men show no such adaptation and lose their reproductive capacity more gradually and later in life. Children can survive if their father dies because the father invests less energy in rearing the young than the mother. Menopause is an adaptation necessary only for women and prevents the production of children for whom maternal care is not insured because of the mother's advanced age. Symons (1979), who labels the above "the Jewish Mother Theory of Menopause," provides a very similar explanation but denies that menopause is an adaptation. He views it as an "artifact" of the relatively recent increased life span of human populations and "the much greater physiological expenditure female fertility entails" (Symons 1979: 14).

Differential parental investment by males and females is also at the core of Gaulin's (1980) explanation of "sexual dimorphism" in later life. Using cross-cultural ratings on contemporary societies, Gaulin suggests that male parental investment as well as male parental certainty increased as mankind abandoned hunting and turned to cultivation. Male parental investment in the form of heritable wealth can be used even after a father's death. Female parental investment, on the other hand, consists of maternal care, which ceases at a mother's death. Gaulin views the inability of women to bear children late in life as a possible adaptive response to differences in male and female parental investment.

Ruse (1979) suggests that the postreproductive years are better spent helping grandchildren than producing children whose survival to maturity is unlikely because of the mother's age. Yet, according to the cross-cultural evidence (Apple 1956, Bart 1979), grandparenting behavior is not a constant. Sociobiology suggests that, unlike grandmothering behavior toward the offspring of a daughter, grandmothering behavior toward the putative offspring of a son would depend upon the degree of male parental certainty which can be ascribed to children (James Dow, personal communication 1980). Although variations in male parental certainty have been assessed by Gaulin (1980), such hypotheses cannot be tested until there are cross-cultural ratings of grandmothering behavior. Since such behavior is a variable without a universal definition, it seems unlikely to be responsible for human survival.

Alexander (1974) suggests the importance of post-reproductive females as "repositories of information." However, he notes that menopause evolved as women survived to ages at which the production of additional offspring was less "profitable" than insuring the mating success of those children they had already borne. This shift in effort was the result of the hierarchical ranking of older females in highly polygynous societies. (Alexander suggests that our remote ancestors lived in such a society.) Maternal rank determined the rank of the offspring, and high rank insured greater mating success. By political maneuvering, a mother could insure the entry of her male offspring into the breeding population and thus increase her own reproductive success through the insured production of grandchildren.

Among these authors, Alexander is the most imaginative and suggests a possible evolutionary origin for a portion of the cross-cultural evidence: the fact that women typically become eligible for achieved statuses and recognition beyond the household after their childbearing years. There is no compelling reason that being a midwife, a mistress of ceremonies at initiation, a curer, or a holy woman is incompatible with the care of young children.[8] Perhaps postponement of such special positions did confer advantages on the mature children of these women during mankind's distant past. A recent work by Gould (1978) dealing with the psychology of adulthood urges women in the middle years to take charge of their lives, to gain a new vision of the self and the world. For Gould this period in the lives of women should be seen as a period of action and expansion, a time "to experience a broader range of social contacts and to expand their own personalities" (Gould 1978: 266). Gould's views and the cross-cultural evidence suggest that Alexander's formulations are not without support, although the mating success of offspring is not necessarily the major motive for achievement in middle-aged women.

Parenting behavior and species survival. Species survival and adaptation are also central to the hypotheses of Gutmann (1975, 1977), which provide the fullest explanation of the cross-cultural evidence. For Gutmann, parenthood is the pivotal life-cycle experience. The relative uniformity of sex roles in all societies is the result of the panhuman demands of parenthood. Behaviors which are defined as masculine and feminine are crucial for parenting behavior, and hence for the survival of the species, in providing physical and emotional security for the young. Female behavior minimizes aggressiveness because if it were turned upon the offspring it might hurt or destroy them. Furthermore, aggressiveness might antagonize the male upon whom the mother and children depend. Males, in turn, must give up dependent behavior during what Gutmann calls the "parenting emergency." Once child rearing is completed, members of both sexes are free to indulge in behaviors which they have had to deny themselves previously. Species survival no longer depends upon masculine behavior by males and feminine behavior by females. For Gutmann, the definitions of these behaviors depend as much upon age as upon sex. Women must exhibit feminine behavior while being parents and can later lapse into "masculine" behavior, and the reverse is true for men.

Gutmann's hypotheses suggest an explanation for the fact that older women are viewed as being "like men" in many societies (see Griffen 1977, Bart 1969, Kerns 1979). It also explains why restrictions of many kinds are lifted and why indecorous behavior is overlooked for "shameless old ladies." It suggests why assertiveness and dominance are possible in the relations with sons, daughters, daughters-in-law, sons-in-law, and even aged husbands, and why an ambitious woman can eventually aspire to achievement and recognition.

Although psychoanalytic theory, sociobiology, Whiting's formulations concerning assigned settings, and the universal physiological changes ushered in by middle age account for portions of the evidence, Gutmann's hypotheses provide the most satisfactory explanation. My own interpretation complements Gutmann's, also stressing parenthood but suggesting no parallel in the roles of the sexes in later life. I stress the importance of being the mother of adult children.

Relationship with adult children. Data on nonhuman primates (see, e.g., Lancaster 1976) provide strong evidence for a mother-offspring bond which not only lasts through life, but strongly influences the behavior of the individual and the social organization of the group. The pervasiveness of this relationship suggests that it is part of primate adaptation. Yet the enduring nature of the mother-child bond among humans remains obscure because of the insistent preoccupation of the social sciences with the mothering of the young. The ethnographic data on the relationship, once offspring are adult, is consequently sketchy. The powerful coalition of mothers and adult sons is frequently reported, however, for patrilocal societies, and even for matrilocal ones, very few of which practice village exogamy. The relationship between mothers and adult daughters is less fully described.

The ethnographic literature does clearly indicate that in many societies the survival of offspring to adulthood is something of a triumph because of the high mortality rates for infants, children, and youth. (LeVine 1977 reports that infant mortality alone reaches 60 percent in parts of West Africa.) Whether viewed as evidence of achievement or of good fortune, adult offspring enhance the position of their parents and contribute to their well-being.

Apparently without exception, ideals of behavior in all societies dictate support, deference, and respect for mothers by their grown children, whereas norms which govern the relationship between siblings, in-laws and spouses and even that between fathers and offspring show much greater variation. These are ideals, and we know from our own society, Mother's Day notwithstanding, that the actual behavior of adult children may deviate considerably. Yet the apparent universality of such ideals is striking.

In a number of societies, the bond with adult offspring is reinforced by the mother's continuing right to dispense food within the household. This control of the larder symbolizes the mother's role as the earliest love object and provider of food and nurturance. The association between mother and food is celebrated in a memorable passage in Schneider's study of American kinship: "the first step in understanding mothers is in understanding the special place food has in the family" (Schneider 1968: 15). The mother's continuing control of food in the household appears as a theme in Roy's account of upper-class Bengali women, Mernissi's account of Moslem Morocco, Richards' account of the Bemba, Murphy and Murphy's account of the Mundurucu, and my own account of the Iroquois.

Conclusion

The mother-offspring bond is lifelong, part of the panprimate heritage reinforced by ideals of behavior which are apparently universal and, in some societies, by the continuing association of mother and food. This enhanced status for older women is separate from their roles as widows, mothers-in-law, grandmothers, curers, midwives, and religious specialists. In some societies, being the mother of adult children contrasts dramatically with an earlier restricted and powerless life. Degrees of discontinuity can be accounted for by variations in the rules of inheritance as well as by variations in the separateness of the sexes in daily life. Societies in which such aloofness is marked provide older women with the additional crucial role of intermediary between the worlds of men and women. In other societies, there is less contrast in the position of older and younger women. Regardless of the role society assigns to women in the childbearing years, a powerful constellation of innate behavior, affect, and symbolism enhances the position of mothers of adult children, freeing them from previous restrictions, giving them authority over certain kinsmen, and providing them opportunities for achievement and recognition.

Even in our society, writers and thinkers have recognized the social status of older women with adult sons. For the mother of his college friend, John Donne wrote:

> No spring nor summer beauty hath such grace
> As I have seen in one autumnal face. . .
> If 'twere a shame to love, here 'twere no shame;
> Affection here takes reverence's name. . . .
> In all her words to every hearer fit
> You may at revels, or at council sit.

Ninth Elegie, "The Autumnal"

Notes

1. From *Current Anthropology*, Volume 23, no. 2 (April 1982). Reprinted by permission of the University of Chicago Press. I would like to thank my colleagues Peter Bertocci, James Dow, Nahum Medalia, and Shelagh O'Rourke for their kindness in making a variety of materials available to me. I thank also those who generously gave me preprints, reprints, and bibliographic suggestions for use in this paper: Jean Briggs, Donna Lee Davis, Marcha Flint, David Gutmann, Patricia Kaufert, Alice Kehoe, Virginia Kerns, Jane Lancaster, Douglas Raybeck, Jacqueline Solway, and Anne Wright. I gratefully acknowledge the support of Oakland University Faculty Research Grant in my work on portions of this paper.

2. For cross-cultural studies of menopause and menopausal symptoms, consult Flint (1975, 1978), Dougherty (1978), Dowty et al. (1970), Goodman (1980), Maoz et al. (1978), Wright (1979a) and the bibliographic essay by Kerns (1980).

3. The response to menopause and middle age within Western society varies among ethnic groups (for example, see Dowty et al. 1970, Maoz et al. 1978, Goodman 1980, Flint 1978, Wright 1979b) as well as among individuals (for example, see Neugart 1968, Grossman and Bart 1979).

4. Whether this alleged sexual voracity on the part of women is projection or wish fulfillment on the part of male informants or a reality remains a matter of conjecture.

5. For a review of this controversy and a reassessment of the evidence, see Dow (1979, 1980).

6. Cosminsky (1976) reports that most midwives are elderly. Government training programs typically produce young midwives. Formal training may place them in a supervisory position above the elderly, traditional practitioner, but the credibility of the young woman in the community will be undermined if she is unmarried or without children of her own.

7. For commentary on the psychoanalytic view of aging

women, see Dowty et al. (1970), Bruck (1979), and Grossman and Bart (1979).

8. However, Spring (1978: 186) writes of the Luvale of Zambia: "To specialize in women's cures is tedious and time-consuming, and women actively involved with the day-to-day tasks of child care and pregnancy are not able to do this."

References Cited

Albert, Ethel
1963 Women of Burundi: A Study of Social Values. *In* Women of Tropical Africa. Denise Paulme, ed., H. M. Wright, trans. pp. 179-215. Berkeley and Los Angeles: University of California Press.

Alexander, Richard D.
1974 The Evolution of Social Behavior. Annual Review of Ecology and Systematics 5:325-383.

Apoko, Anna
1967 At Home in the Village: Growing up in Acholi. *In* East African Childhood: Three Versions. Lorene K. Fox, ed. pp. 45-75. New York: Oxford University Press.

Apple, Dorrian
1956 The Social Structure of Grandparenthood. American Anthropologist 58:656-663.

Barash, David P.
1977 Sociobiology and Behavior. New York: Elsevier.

Bart, Pauline
1969 Why Women's Status Changes in Middle Age: The Turns of the Social Ferris Wheel. Sociological Symposium 3:1-18.

1970 Mother Portnoy's Complaint. Trans-Action 8:69-74.

Bell, Diane
1980 Desert Politics: Choices in the 'Marriage Market.' *In* Women and Colonization: Anthropological Perspectives. Mona Etienne and Eleanor Leacock, eds. pp. 239-269. New York: Praeger/Bergin.

Benedek, Therese
1950 Climacterium: A Developmental Phase. The Psychoanalytic Quarterly. 19:1-27.

Briggs, Jean L.
1974 Eskimo Women: Makers of Men. *In* Many Sisters: Women in Cross-Cultural Perspective. C. Matthiasson, ed., pp. 261-304. New York: Free Press.

Brown, Judith K.
1963 A Cross-Cultural Study of Female Initiation Rites. American Anthropologist 65:837-853.

1970 Economic Organization and the Position of Women Among the Iroquois. Ethnohistory 17:151-167.

1978 The Recruitment of a Female Labor Force. Anthropos 73:41-48.

1979 No Longer Young and Not Yet Old: A Cross-Cultural Exploration of the End of the Child Bearing Years. Paper presented at the meetings of the Third Annual Menstrual Cycle Conference. Tucson.

Bruck, Connie
1979 Menopause. Human Behavior 8:38-46.

Campbell, Bernard
1966 Human Evolution: An Introduction to Man's Adaptations. Chicago: Aldine.

Chagnon, Napoleon A.
1968 Yanomamö: The Fierce People. New York: Holt, Rinehart and Winston.

Chinas, Beverly
1973 The Isthmus Zapotec: Women's Roles in Cultural Context. New York: Holt, Rinehart and Winston.

Cosminsky, Sheila
1976 Cross-Cultural Perspectives on Midwifery. *In* Medical Anthropology. F. X. Grollig, S.J., and H. B. Haley, eds., pp. 229-248. The Hague: Mouton.

Davis, Donna Lee
1979 Women's Status and Experience of Menopause in a Newfoundland Fishing Village. Paper presented at the meetings of the American Anthropological Association. Cincinnati.

Dawkins, Richard
1976 The Shellfish Gene. New York: Oxford University Press.

Deutsch, Helene
1945 The Psychology of Women: A Psychoanalytic Interpretation. Vol. II: Motherhood. New York: Grune and Stratton.

Divale, William and Marvin Harris
1976 Population, Warfare, and the Male Supremacist Complex. American Anthropologist 78:521-538.

Dougherty, Molly C.
1978 An Anthropological Perspective on Aging and Women in the Middle Years. *In* The Anthropology of Health. Eleanor E. Bauwens, ed., pp. 167-176. St. Louis: C. V. Mosby.

Dow, James
1979 Women Capture as a Motivation for Warfare. Paper presented at the meetings of the American Anthropological Association. Cincinnati.

1980 The Male Supremacist Complex: Current Critique and Re-evaluation of Evidence. Paper presented at the meetings of the Central States Anthropological Society. Ann Arbor, Michigan.

Dowty, Nancy, B. Maoz, A. Antonovsky, and H. Wijsenbeek
1970 Climacterium in Three Cultural Contexts. Tropical and Geographical Medicine 22:77-86.

Dwyer, Daisy Hilse
1978 Ideologies of Sexual Inequality and Strategies for Change in Male-Female Relations. American Ethnologist 5:227-240.

Erikson, Erik H.
1950 Childhood and Society. New York: W. W. Norton.

Faithorn, Elizabeth
1976 Women as Persons: Aspects of Female Life and Male-Female Relations Among the Kafe. *In* Man and Woman in the New Guinea Highlands. Paula Brown and Georgeda Buchbinder, eds., pp. 86-95. Washington, DC: Special Publications of the American Anthropological Association No. 8.

Flint, Marcha
1975 The Menopause: Reward or Punishment? Psychosomatics 16:161-163.

1978 Transcultural Influences in Peri-Menopause. Paper presented at the International Symposium on Psychosomatics in Peri-Menopause. Utrecht, Holland.

Friedl, Ernestine
1967 The Position of Women: Appearance and Reality. Anthropological Quarterly 40: 97-108.

Gaulin, S. J. C.
1980 Sexual Dimorphism on Human Post-Reproductive Life Span: Possible Causes. Journal of Human Evolution 9:227-232.

Goodman, Madeleine
1980 Toward a Biology of Menopause. Signs 5:739-753.

Goody, Jack
1976 Production and Reproduction: A Comparative Study of the Domestic Domain. New York: Cambridge University Press.

Gould, Roger
1978 Transformations: Growth and Change in Adult Life. New York: Simon and Schuster.

Griffen, Joyce
1977 A Cross-Cultural Investigation of Behavioral Changes at Menopause. Social Science Journal 14:49-55.

Grossman, Marilyn, and Paula Bart
1979 Taking the Men Out of Menopause. *In* Women Look at Biology Looking at Women. Ruth Hubbard, Mary Sue Henifin and Barbara Fried, eds., pp. 163-185. Cambridge, Massachusetts: Schenkman.

Gutmann, David
1975 Parenthood: A Key to the Comparative Study of the Life Cycle. *In* Life Span Developmental Psychology: Normative Life Crises. N. Datan and L. Ginsberg, eds., pp. 167-184. New York: Academic Press.

1977 The Cross-Cultural Perspective: Notes toward a Comparative Psychology of Aging. *In* Handbook of the Psychology of Aging. J. Birren and K. Schaie, eds., pp. 302-326. New York: Van Nostrand.

Hamilton, Annette
1970 The Role of Women in Aboriginal Marriage Arrangements. *In* Woman's Role in Aboriginal Society. Fay Gale, ed., pp. 17-20. Canberra: Australian Institute of Aboriginal Studies. Australian Aboriginal Studies No. 36, Social Anthropology Series No. 6.

Hayes, Rose Oldfield
1975 Female Genital Mutilation, Fertility Control, Women's Roles, and the Patrilineage in Modern Sudan: A Functional Analysis. American Ethnologist 2:617-633.

Henry, Jules
1977 Forty-Year Old Jitters in Married Urban Women. *In* Annual Editions (1966): Readings in Anthropology 77/78. David Rosen et al., eds., pp. 262-268. Guilford, Connecticut: Dushkin.

Hungry Wolf, Beverly
1980 The Ways of My Grandmothers. New York: Morrow.

Kaufert, Patricia
1979 The Menopause as a Life Crisis Event. Paper presented at the meetings of the Society for Applied Anthropology. Philadelphia.

Kehoe, Alice B.
1976 Old Woman Had Great Power. The Western Canadian Journal of Anthropology 6:68-76.

Kerns, Virginia
1979 Social Transition at Menopause. Paper presented at the meetings of the American Anthropological Association. Cincinnati.

1980 Menopause and the Post-Reproductive Years. National Women's Anthropology Newsletter 4(2):15-16, 4(3):26-27.

Kolenda, Pauline
1978 Caste in Contemporary India: Beyond Organic Solidarity. Menlo Park, California: Benjamin/Cummings.

Lancaster, Jane B.
1976 Sex Roles in Primate Societies. *In* Sex Differences: Social and Biological Perspectives. M. Teitelbaum, ed., pp. 22-61. New York: Doubleday/Anchor.

Leacock, Eleanor
1978 Women's Status in Egalitarian Society: Implications for Social Evolution. Current Anthropology 19:247-275.

Lee, Richard B.
1981 In Praise of Older Women: Work, Sexuality, and Aging Among !Kung Women. Paper presented at the annual meeting of the Canadian Ethnological Society, Ottawa, Ontario.

LeVine, Robert
1977 Child Rearing as Cultural Adaptation. *In* Culture and Infancy: Variations in the Human Experience. P. Leiderman, S. Tulkin, and A. Rosenfeld, eds., pp. 15-27. New York: Academic Press.

Lewis, Oscar
1941 Manly-Hearted Women Among the North Piegan. American Anthropologist 43:173-187.

Lowenthal, Marjorie Fiske, Majda Thurnher, and David Chiriboga
1975 Four States of Life: A Comparative Study of Women and Men Facing Transitions. San Francisco: Jossey-Bass.

Maoz, Benjamin, Aaron Antonovsky, Alan Apter, Nancy Datan, Joseph Hochberg, and Yetta Salomon
1978 The Effect of Outside Work on the Menopausal Woman. Maturitas 1:43-53.

Marshall, Gloria
1964 Women, Trade and the Yoruba Family. Unpublished Ph.D. dissertation, Columbia University.

Marshall, Lorna, and Megan Biesele
1974 N/um Tchai: The Ceremonial Dance of the !Kung Bushmen. A Study Guide. Somerville, Massachusetts: Documentary Educational Resources.

Mead, Margaret
1949 Male and Female: A Study of the Sexes in a Changing World. New York: Morrow.

Mernissi, Fatima
1975 Beyond the Veil: Male-Female Dynamics in a Modern Muslim Society. Cambridge, Massachusetts: Schenkman.

Michaelson, Evalyn Jacobson, and Walter Goldschmidt
1971 Female Roles and Male Dominance Among Peasants. Southwestern Journal of Anthropology 27:330-352.

Morsy, Soheir
1978 Sex Roles, Power, and Illness in an Egyptian Village. American Ethnologist 5:137-150.

Murphy, Yolanda, and Robert Murphy
1974 Women of the Forest. New York: Columbia University Press.

Neugarten, Bernice, ed.
1968 Middle Age and Aging: A Reader in Social Psychology. Chicago: University of Chicago Press.

Paul, Lois, and Benjamin Paul
1975 The Maya Midwife as a Sacred Specialist: A Guatemalan Case. American Ethnologist 2:707-726.

Quinn, Naomi
1977 Anthropological Studies on Women's Status. Annual Review of Anthropology 6:181-225.

Ramos, Alcida
1979 On Women's Status in Yanoama Societies. Current Anthropology 20:185-187.

Raybeck, Douglas
1979 The Ideal and the Real: The Status of Women in Kelantan Malay Society. Paper presented at the meetings of the Northeastern Anthropological Association. Henniker, New Hampshire.

Richard, Audrey
1956 Chisungu: A Girls' Initiation Ceremony Among the Bemba of Northern Rhodesia. New York: Grove Press.

Rosaldo, Michelle Z.
1974 Women, Culture, and Society: A Theoretical Overview. *In* Women, Culture, and Society. M. Rosaldo and L. Lamphere, eds., pp. 17-42. Stanford, California: Stanford University Press.

Roy, Manisha
1975 Bengali Women. Chicago: University of Chicago Press.

Ruse, Michael
1979 Sociobiology: Sense or Nonsense. Boston: D. Reidel/Pallas Paperbacks.

Sacks, Karen
1976 State Bias and Women's Status. American Anthropologist 78:565-569.

1979 Sisters and Wives: The Past and Future of Sexual Equality. Westport, Connecticut: Greenwood Press.

Schneider, David M.
1968 American Kinship: A Cultural Account. Englewood Cliffs, New Jersey: Prentice-Hall.

Shapiro, Judith
1980 *Review of* the Evolution of Human Sexuality, by Donald Symons. Science 207:1193-1194.

Skultans, V.
1970 The Symbolic Significance of Menstruation and the Menopause. Man 5:639-651.

Spring, Anita
1978 Epidemiology of Spirit Possession among the Luvale of Zambia. *In* Women in Ritual and Symbolic Roles. Judith Hoch-Smith and Anita Spring, eds. pp. 165-190. New York: Plenum.

Srinivas, M.N.
1977 The Changing Position of Indian Women. Man 12:221-238.

Symons, Donald
1979 The Evolution of Human Sexuality. New York: Oxford University Press.

Tiffany, Sharon W.
1980 Anthropology and the Study of Women. American Anthropologist 82:374-380.

Whiting, Beatrice
1980 Culture and Social Behavior: A Model for the Development of Social Behavior. Ethos 8:95-116.

Whiting, John W., M., and Beatrice Whiting
1975 Aloofness and Intimacy of Husbands and Wives: A Cross-Cultural Study. Ethos 3:183-207.

Wright, Anne
1979a Roles and the Cultural Interpretation of Menopause. Paper presented at the meetings of the American Anthropological Association. Cincinnati.

1979b Variation in Navaho Menopause: Toward an Explanation. Paper presented at the Third Annual Menstrual Cycle Conference. Tucson.

Wolf, Margery
1974 Chinese Women: Old Skills in a New Context. *In* Women, Culture, and Society. M. Rosaldo and L. Lamphere, eds., pp. 157-172. Stanford, California: Stanford University Press.

Yang, C. K.
1959 A Chinese Village in Early Communist Transition. Cambridge, Massachusetts: The MIT Press.

Working for the Phone Company: New Careers for Women?

Kathlyn C. Zahniser

I am a female and when I was hired by the telephone company in February 1974 I did not realize the obstacles I would encounter. I remained in that company's employ until my resignation in September 1976. When I now review my experiences as a female blue-collar worker I am amazed at my initial naiveté. During my employment I was certain I could change the system; the only thing I actually changed was my own perception of myself as a woman. My resignation was prompted by the realization that I had been fighting a losing battle. In the following paper I try to narrate specific events that depict the female role in a blue-collar world.

I was originally hired by the telephone company as a lineman and it was a job I retained for one year. I remember being very pleased and grateful that a large corporation had offered me the opportunity and responsibility of a well-paying job. To start, I was sent out of town to the Training Center for a four-week training session. After that, I would be assigned a permanent work location.

The manifest function of the program at the Training Center was to initiate the employee into his or her new craft job. A craft job is one that requires a certain amount of skill and training. As such, the pay scale is considerably higher than the non-craft jobs. Although employee initiation was the manifest goal, the latent function of the Training Center was to weed out those employees who could not pass the pole-climbing requirement.

The four-week program consisted of First Aid, Basic Electricity, Driver Training and Pole-Climbing. A great deal of emphasis was placed on pole-climbing; in fact, the other three courses filled in the gaps between the climbing sessions. If by the end of the four weeks an employee could not climb a pole properly, safely, and confidently, then he or she was either terminated or sent back to the position of employment from which he or she had come, within the company.

At the beginning of the school, there were fifteen men and seven women trainees. By the end, two of the men and four of the women had dropped out. Ineptitude at pole-climbing was the reason in every case. Two of the women failed the actual pole-climbing for the usual reason, fear of heights. It is not hard to understand this reason. One climbs a pole with just your "hooks," portable leg irons with a small barb near the instep of the foot. The barb at the end of your hook penetrates the pole a mere quarter of an inch. The instructors kept telling us that these could support the weight of a normal adult because of a law of physics. I suppose that is true, but when you are eighteen feet straight up you really *have* to believe that it is true, and that the barbs are working as the law prescribes they should.

A favorite training exercise at the Center was to have everyone climb up a pole about ten feet or so off the ground and toss a basketball around to each other. The ball is not just tossed; it is hurled. Some of the men made it their objective to knock each other off the pole. If one missed the ball, then you had to climb down the pole to retrieve it. This "game" was designed to build your confidence and allow you to relax on a telephone pole. I found it to be the opposite and altogether quite frightening.

In any event, two of the women did not make it through that particular training exercise. The other two women were forced to drop out because of a frustrating technicality. Before you climb a pole with just your "hooks," you must first practice on the "step-pole." A step-pole is a telephone pole that has permanent steps hammered into the sides so that a person can climb it like a ladder. For public safety, the first two steps are detachable. They are ordinarily detached, absent, so that children cannot climb the pole easily and possibly get hurt. The telephone employee is provided with a pair of "butt-steps," brackets attached to the pole to serve as the first two steps in the ladder. The lower butt-step is three feet off the ground. The other two women who failed pole-climbing were just under five feet tall. It was physically impossible for them to reach that first step and still keep the other foot on the ground. They could reach the three-foot step if they jumped a little. There were always several ways of doing any of the tasks, but the supervisors felt that a jump up to the first step, so that both feet were off the ground, presented a safety hazard that could not be tolerated. It was rather sad to see the two women straining to almost reach the first step.

At the Training Center I made a puzzling discovery; I discovered that all the men had been assigned a work location already, and some had even been on the job for as much as two months. None of the women knew where she was to be sent or had any idea of what her actual job might entail. I conjecture that it might have had to do with the pole-climbing requirement. Fewer women made it through the pole-climbing training than did men. When I attended the school, more than half of the women--four out of seven--were forced to drop out on that account. The company may have hesitated in assigning women to jobs until a woman could prove that she could climb telephone poles. Since the failure rate among men was much lower, the company could be fairly certain that most men would pass and could be assigned to a job in advance of training.

When I finished my training, I was anxious to see what my real job would be like. I was apprehensive, nervous and ignorant; I could not even distinguish between the telephone cables and the electric company's cables on a telephone pole. As a lineman, I thought I would be working on a line-gang stringing telephone cable--a rather romantic notion, as it turned out. Oddly enough, I never worried about being a woman in a male-dominated field. I was more worried about fitting into a blue-collar setting. My only previous exposure to "real" blue-collar workers had come about with barhopping and drinking beer in blue-collar bars. I expected my co-workers to be relatively uneducated, hard-living good ol' boys. I did not experience any animosity from them while in their bars and I expected the same from them on the job once they discovered that I was just one of the guys.

My first day on the job was quite an experience. I reported to my job location at the appointed time. My boss, Sam Anderson, was an old salt. He was never without a cigar in his mouth, and his skin was red and weathered. In his fifties, with a shock of white hair, Sam's entire wardrobe consisted of khaki slacks and several different shirts. His vocabulary closely resembled his attire in size and eloquence. His first words to me were, "God damn, it's a God damned WOMAN!" I realized later that until I actually appeared, he had no way of knowing that I was female since the employment roster listed my first and middle names in initial form. Within an hour's time I was traded back to my "original" crew. It seems that before I had arrived (while I was still presumed to be a male) I was traded to Sam's crew. My "original" boss was to receive the next two new employees. Sam's crew, however, was shorthanded at the time and needed a new employee, so he had asked Bob for one of the new crewmen. Sam was furious with the trade and felt certain that he had been tricked. He thought that Bob Moore, my original boss, had known all along that I was a woman. Sam immediately marched into Bob's office and demanded that the trade be called off. He would never be so shorthanded that he had to take a woman! At the time, I did not mind the trade back to Bob. I certainly did not want to work for anyone who did not want me.

When I joined Bob Moore's crew, there were three other members, two Mexican-Americans and one white Navy veteran. Bob had been a foreman for only a short time and he was an eager and enthusiastic boss. I credit to him my relatively lengthy term of employment. The more I worked for Bob, the more I respected him and liked him personally. He was encouraging and often told me that he did not care if I was a woman because everyone deserved a fair chance. Bob maintained this same attitude throughout my assignment with him.

The training school gave no specific experience relating directly to the job; rather the new employees are trained on the job by the experienced crew members. It was a new crew, and we had to share trucks and tools until new supplies arrived. I began my work riding with Victor and Ray, the two Chicano crew members. Two weeks after I arrived, the crew received another member named Ron. Actually, the old crew members knew he was coming; in fact, they knew him because he had worked on the crew for a week before he was sent to school. Our crew now consisted of five young and, for the most part, inexperienced members headed by an enthusiastic boss.

The job was turning into a career for me. I was more than eager to learn and I became absolutely fascinated with telephone technology. I had no idea I could learn a craft skill and even join a union. At first, the work was often strenuous and tiring. I started out physically weak, but within a month or so my strength had increased substantially. I was able to do the heavier tasks with relative ease and could hold my own with the other crew members. It was my observation, however, that the men used as little strength as possible while I would often attempt tasks they would not consider. On one occasion I very nearly hurt my back trying to do the impossible. Two other men and I were sent to another work center to pick up some cable off a huge cable reel. I asked the other two men what I could do to help and they told me to move the cable reel to another spot. Not until my back began to feel the strain did I realize that the two were laughing at me. Nobody moves a cable reel alone since it weighs several thousand pounds.

During my first three months, my job was a pleasure. My self-confidence increased, and I felt I was making some remarkable friendships with my colleagues. I was dependent upon them to train me correctly; otherwise, my job could have been in jeopardy. I knew my job hinged upon compatibility. I also believed that even if I was not the best lineman that ever lived, I would never be fired for not trying. And try I did. I was the last one to come back to the garage at the end of the day, the one who worked through lunch and coffee breaks, and the one who never left the job site to run around.

I soon noticed that two crew mates, Ron and Jim, were becoming less friendly to me. They had been riding together due to the tool and truck shortage. I, on the other hand, had a new van and all new tools (prized possessions). I was sufficiently trained to do some work by myself. Ron was short of equipment, but I did not think he minded all that much. It is infinitely more entertaining to work with a partner than by yourself. Ron was civil to me, but restrained. Jim was the one who was becoming hostile. I did not exactly understand what was happening and our relationship deteriorated rapidly. I remained pleasant, but perplexed at the turn of events. I finally became silent and spoke to Jim only when he spoke first. After a month, I was quite distressed. The rest of the crew was friendly, but I could not imagine how I had offended Jim. I had taken such precautions to be a wonderfully cheery person. Eventually, Jim and I came to blows. I responded angrily to Jim's last insult. I made it clear that I did not understand what he was doing and asked him not to bother speaking to me again. I was surprised to see a look of mild shock on his face, especially since I was not all that threatening. I only wished to be left alone. For two weeks I neither spoke to Jim nor acknowledged his presence. Not long after that, Jim apologized to me and tried to explain his behavior. Ron was becoming one of Jim's best friends and he was indignant over the injustice he perceived. He felt that I did not deserve new tools or a new truck since I was a girl. The tools would be better served if Ron had received them first. Fortunately, my boss worked on the seniority principle. I had one week's service over Ron and would always receive new supplies before him. The confrontation was helpful. Jim and I were able to discuss the nature of sex-roles and it became an enlightening experience for both of us. We became very good friends--much to my relief. I did, however, become painfully aware of the fact that I was still a woman in a traditional male job. I had been too trusting and naive.

Throughout the year that I had the lineman's job there is one experience that stands out from the rest. It was the hardest lesson of all for me, but a worthwhile lesson at that. At the time I was working as a cable inspector which is a glorified title for a mere observer. The telephone company puts most of the new cable underground. To do this job, a contracting company is hired. The cable inspector watches the contractor to make sure the new cable is placed twenty-four inches or more into the ground. My job at the time was just such a task. The contractor I was watching was digging the trench for the cable with a backhoe, which is like a huge mechanized shovel. The new trench was next to an existing underground cable. The existing cable had already been flagged so we knew where it was and could tell exactly where not to dig. It is very important not to dig up existing cable since it knocks customers out of service. For several days I had been having some trouble with this particular contractor. He did not seem to pay very much attention to what I told him. Actually, I was not very bossy; I asked him very politely to do things. He usually ignored me. On this particular day he was coming very close to the existing cable. I asked him again to dig in another direction that was not quite so close to the old cable. He just glared at me and continued on. The inevitable happened. He pulled up the working cable out of the ground and knocked it out of service. It was dangling in half, right in front of my eyes. I was very angry, but I did not know what to do. He was angry at me for being right. Within a half hour a telephone company cable repairman appeared. He was furious. He immediately turned to me and said, "You God damned woman! What the hell's the matter with you? Why weren't you watching this guy? I bet you've got a mattress in the back of that van and you were back there fucking!" I was at a loss for words. It was my fault, but he did not need to be quite so dramatic. There was not too much time to brood over the matter because my supervisor showed up. Whenever a cable has been cut, a supervisor always shows up. It is as if they have a sixth sense. Bob was very perceptive and he knew that I had been having trouble with this particular contractor. After I explained what had happened, he walked over to the contractor and said, "Get off that backhoe, load it up and get off this job. My inspector is the telephone company as far as you are concerned, and she is your boss. She asked you to do the job the right way and you refused. You are now fired and you will never work for the phone company again." Bob then walked back over to where I was standing and said, "See, K.C. This is how it is done. Contractors work for you, and if they don't do what you want, then fire them." I had no idea that I could actually fire a bad contractor. I thought that I just had to put up with them until the job was finished. I had not wanted to cause any trouble, but by not being assertive I had caused a great deal of trouble. On one hand, I was truly upset by what the cable repairman had said to me; but on the other, I was very excited. I had found a small piece of power within myself that I never knew existed.

I was in the lineman's job for a year. At the beginning of 1975, the telephone company was required to place more minorities in Cable Splicer positions. The Equal Employment Opportunity Commission had filed a complaint against the company and they were heading towards court. Through the shifting of paperwork, Ray, Victor and I assumed instant Cable Splicer titles. Under normal circumstances, the Communication Workers of America handles the placing of employees in job vacancies by seniority bidding. In other words, if an employee wanted to bid on the splicing job and had more seniority than the other bidders, he would be offered the job first provided he were qualified. In this case, the union was completely ignored because of the lawsuit. It caused some friction between the minorities and the whites.

At first, I refused the splicing job. I felt that the company was fulfilling the obligation only through emergency action and was not honestly trying to rectify the situation. I was satisfied with my present job, and I enjoyed working for Bob. I knew there would be some backlash from trying to equalize the minorities' position. I did realize that if I ever wanted to be a Cable Splicer later on, my chances would be slim. I knew it was difficult for a woman to be placed into the higher-paying jobs. As the job gets better in the phone company, fewer females are found. Seniority was also a criterion for this type of job. I had no intention of putting in ten years as a lineman just to move up to a cable splicer. As it was, I was a bit bored with my present job.

Higher company officials visited with me in an attempt to persuade me to take the job. I was told that my work was appreciated greatly. The new job was much more skilled and challenging, and I was the perfect candidate. The interview ended with, "I wish you would consider the job. We'd love to have you." How could I refuse? Thus, my first year as a lineman ended and I became a cable splicer.

My new boss, Jack Turner, was considerably different from Bob Moore. He was not sympathetic to my job enthusiasm. He viewed women on the job as an evil necessary to keep his job. He admitted freely that women had no business working in an outside job. He frequently commented that a man and a woman could not work side by side out in the field without becoming sexually involved with each other. For Jack, that was the natural course of things. He was never convinced otherwise.

Jack went out of his way to humiliate his female crew members. The number of women on his crew varied. At one time there were four of us, but within a year's time the number was down to two. Two of the women were forced to resign on technicalities. One girl overslept one morning and did not call in. This is a grave offense and if the supervisor chooses, he can indefinitely suspend the employee. This is a nice way of firing someone. That is what Jack did in this case. But on another occasion, I observed Jack phoning one of the male crew members at home when he did not show up for work. Jack just laughed and commented on how it was so typical for this employee to do something like that. The other woman was forced to resign because she refused to do a particular job. Again, this is a rather ambiguous decision on the supervisor's part. Unfortunately, he really disliked this employee. She was radical in her politics and in her views on women's liberation. Not only did Jack dislike her, the whole male crew disliked her. She was shunned by all of the males. I promised myself not to fall into the same trap. Keeping one's job required compatibility and diplomacy.

Some of Jack's attempts to humiliate me even embarrassed several of the male crew members. Aside from the sexual innuendoes, one of Jack's favorite tricks was to hold up the centerfold of *Hustler* magazine in front of the entire crew as we marched in from work in the afternoon.

Jack would point to the graphic areas and say, "K.C., is this your picture? Did you pose for this?" There was little I could say except something in humor.

Jack also had the habit of asking publicly and privately of any male I was working with if they were getting any on the side. This was a daily occurrence for some time. I am certain his question was designed to embarrass me when it was asked publicly, yet he was sincere when he asked the question in private. He still believed that sexual relations between male and female must occur sometime during the day. I learned of his private inquiries through one of the men I rode with. He confided to me that although he found the question to be humorous at first, he, too was becoming uneasy about Jack's persistence. He felt that there was pressure on him to make good Jack's predictions.

Eventually Jack had to abandon his line of questioning. He placed Kathy, another female crew member, with me, and we worked together for several months. Jack was always worried about sending us out on a job alone knowing that disaster was certain with two women on the job. For Jack, though, it was preferable to a man and a woman driving together. Then, none of the men would have to work with a girl. It was almost treated as a loss of status if you were stuck with a girl for any length of time. Even though Kathy and I were personally liked, we were still considered unable to do complex jobs. Jack made it clear that if he did not harass us, and if he was able to maintain his fair percentage of women on the crew, then he was less likely to receive another minority. He feared that he would be sent a black, or even worse, a black female. Jack did not like unwelcome surprises.

There were several obstacles that Kathy and I encountered. Our work was of good quality. We were both meticulous and concerned with doing the job correctly the first time around. Any shoddiness of the work could be a reason for job dismissal. That did not apply to the men, at least not all the men. Jack did have his favorite crew members. There were several men whose work was far below "quality." "Quality" is a standard set by the telephone company. All their work procedures are standardized and if the job is not done by the specification book, then it is not correct. For some of the men, Jack accepted the fact that someone would have to return to their jobs and make it "quality" or even just make it work. The crew's work was subject to spot checks by a Quality Control Inspector. When I was on Bob's crew,

I was constantly backtracking over other crew members' work, making it a quality job. I do not know why I did this, but I like to think it was because of the fierce competition between the area crews to be the best. On both Bob's and Jack's crew, the Quality Inspector was given one of the jobs I had worked on or one in which Kathy and I had worked. We always received a good review from the Inspector, but we never received any praise from the boss.

In one instance, Kathy and I had finished a job that supplied cable to an unbuilt subdivision. We were responsible for the preparation of the cable, all splicing operations, and the final testing of the cable. Jack always demanded that the cable be tested and proven good from the last leg of the job to the central office. When the job was completed we began another job. Two weeks later, Jack received a telephone call from the frame foreman in the central office. He told Jack that he did not know just what his damn women had done, but we had managed to screw things up. Jack immediately flew into a panic, and asked us to go back and correct whatever we had done wrong. Kathy and I carefully retested every wire in the cable and backtracked all the way to the central office. We finally concurred that the problem might be in the central office. Perhaps the cable was spliced incorrectly inside the vault. Still we could find nothing wrong. We checked our blueprints over and over. It finally dawned on us that there was not anything wrong. The frame foreman had made the mistake. He had been a full one hundred pair off on the frame. All the cables are identified on the main frame or switching station by a number and every pair of wires is identified by a numeric color code. He was not even in the right cable for the subdivision. The cable he was testing was running in the opposite direction. When this error was pointed out, we felt very proud of our work. The foreman never admitted his mistake and only shrugged it off. Kathy and I did feel a bit discouraged that we had not trusted our own judgment. Any of the men would have first argued with the foreman and then would try to find the trouble. Kathy and I had blindly accepted the accusation that we had indeed made some terrible mistake.

After one year of cable splicing, Kathy began to lose interest in her job, but most of all, she lost interest in the company. We were often sent out of town to live in motels since our crew was responsible for all of the small towns surrounding our work location. Some towns were as much as 65 miles away from the work center. One day the company laid down an arbitrary rule that gave Kathy the incentive to quit. Our second-line boss, Jack's boss, handed down an unofficial decree stating that any female not wearing a brassiere would be subject to suspension and/or termination. This was all Kathy needed to quit, which she did one day later. I was never quite sure how they were going to check to see if a woman was wearing a bra. There was a great deal of furor about the ruling, but the company held fast to it as long as they could. Their rationale stated that the bra was for our own protection and was a safety item. It would protect the breasts against splinters in case we should fall from a pole. I never knew how the men were going to protect themselves because they certainly were not going to start wearing bras. Furthermore, we rarely climbed poles in our job. A thin nylon undergarment rationalized as a safety item is an exercise in absurdity. The rule was soon disregarded after another lawsuit was threatened. It was not before I was warned by Jack that I would be subject to suspension for disobeying the rule.

I did have some social life with the crew. When we were out of town, everyone would go to a local tavern after work for a few beers. The wives rarely appeared. Jack's wife and one other crew member's wife showed up occasionally. Most of the time we were out of town for several months at a time. For entertainment we either played poker or went to the local bar. One pattern of behavior startled me. The single men and women would group together for entertainment, but the married men would immediately seek a girlfriend from the town. This happened almost without exception and included the men who were newlyweds. One man on the crew had been married less than two weeks when he sought an extramarital affair. Another waited two months. Many of the men's marriages ended in divorce. In the short time I worked with them six out of the nine male crew members went through a divorce. It seemed as if the affairs were a ritual game with the men, a sort of Russian marriage roulette. Topics of conversation revolved around how their wives would literally shoot them if they were discovered. I am surprised there was so little bloodshed. I made certain that the wives knew me and understood that I posed no threat to them.

After Kathy left, the situation deteriorated quickly between Jack and myself. He had received a new female crew member named Barbara. She was not a welcome addition to the crew and Jack made certain that she knew that from the start. He could often reduce her to tears with his uncalled-for comments. He would always imply that she was stupid. He would swear at her and act exasperated, and then turn around and mention to another male that Barbara had a very large chest. I was as encouraging as I could be to her under the circumstances. I was also grateful to Jack for not tormenting me in the same way he did Barbara. Jack would ask her to do tasks she was not yet trained to do. She was also not the most dedicated person, but she should not have had to be; the men certainly were not all that dedicated. Jack suggested that she resign and find a more suitable job, but Barbara remained as steadfast as she could. She realized that Jack would try whatever he could get away with to remove her from the crew. Barbara did not have the same crew support that I thought I had, so she was all the more vulnerable. Unfortunately for me, Barbara told Jack that she was going to stay as long as I was on the crew. She thought Jack would leave her alone after that. She was wrong. Jack began to focus all of his attention upon me. Suddenly, I could do nothing right. My work was inferior, and the jobs assigned to me were the ones no one else wanted. Jack began checking up on me at the job site and criticized my work even more. A very clever fellow, that Jack. He knew just where to hit me. His whole attitude towards me had changed. The joking was not there anymore. I had been thinking of transferring to another larger town for some time so I put in for a transfer. I never did hear anything from them, although I knew they needed experienced cable splicers.

The final blow came from the personal evaluation that occurred every six months. All of my previous evaluations had been quite favorable. I was considered a hard worker who gave as much as possible. My quality was excellent and my work was good. I was cooperative and got on well with my fellow workers. My last six month review was a negative account of my work. It stated that I was extremely slow in my work and that I could not keep up with the other crew members. There were many jobs that I could not do. I was becoming uncooperative with my fellow workers. In effect, my work was inferior. I knew the report was not true. As much as I disliked Jack personally, I never let it interfere with my job and I had expected the same of him. After reading the review, Jack asked me to sign it so he could send it to the main office. Of course, I signed it. I was so furious I had to hold back tears. By the time I got home that evening I was even more angry. I had been insulted, degraded, and my career marred. Actually, it was not much of a career. I had hoped to be one of the first women to climb their corporate ladder from the bottom. Yet here I was having trouble staying at the bottom. The men were always complaining that the company kept putting college graduates and executive secretaries into outside management positions. These people were always described as "not being able to find their ass from a hole in the ground." I was going to be the self-assured woman who could rise to a management position.

I returned to work the next day and informed Jack that I had no intention of letting that evaluation carry my name on it. It was too late. I still could not undo what had been done. He allowed me to make my comments in the margin and I did. Somehow, I felt that they were not going to make a great deal of difference, especially not in the margin. I was certain the transfer office would turn me down after reading my review. After I quit, I moved to the larger town and reapplied to the telephone company. I was offered all types of craft jobs immediately, every job except as a cable splicer. I knew they were short of females in the other positions and they were actively pursuing any hopefuls. Minorities do look nice on paper. At any rate, I recognized the reason why I was hired in each circumstance, and my work record had nothing to do with it.

Barbara was doomed the minute I sent in my resignation. By a stroke of luck another foreman needed a woman on his crew and Jack sent her over. He was ecstatic. He now had no women on his crew. It had taken him a year and a half but he did it. In later contacts Barbara told me how much happier she was in her job and her attitude had really changed. Her new boss was a tolerable fellow. She began to enjoy her work and was able to fend for herself. Best of all, she began to receive favorable reviews and was training a new male employee.

As for myself, I was very disillusioned at the turn of events. I felt that I had no choice but to move to the other city. My pride and self-esteem were practically destroyed. I did not even trust my male colleagues, although there were some who were honestly sympathetic. I was very angry at the organization that allowed men like Jack to have such a responsible job. He was able to point out that women were not able to handle the job. None had stayed for very long and Jack felt that they were irresponsible. Jack had high hopes that the company officials would see their folly and recognize the fact that training women for a craft job was a waste of time and money. Perhaps the EEOC could also be convinced that they were on the wrong track by forcing companies to place women in men's jobs. Jack was right for a while. Through occasional correspondence with crew members I discovered that Jack did not receive another minority for over a year. But when he did, his worst fears came true. He was sent a black female. I understand she was rather tough and that Jack was a little afraid of her.

This paper was not designed to be an expose of the telephone company, but rather an attempt to describe the problematic nature of changing sex-roles. It is my contention that these events (of which only a few were selected) are not isolated and are not specific to the phone company. The economics, politics and ideology of sex roles presents a powerful barrier to the female in this society. Kathy received a great deal of respect after she proved she could handle the job, but then again, her father was a regional vice-president for the phone company. I suspect that Jack tolerated me because of my friendship with Kathy. I knew he liked me personally, but he could never separate me as an employee from me as a woman.

In conclusion, my employment with the phone company is one of the most memorable aspects of my life. It was the most enjoyable, as well as the most disappointing, of all my work experiences. It is unfortunate that the material in this paper was not gathered for a specific academic study. The problem of changing sex roles is a field that needs exploration and study. Traditional male and female job categories are shifting rapidly and as was pointed out in the paper, some men find it difficult to accept the fact. They, in turn, make it impossible for the female worker. Jack persisted in his belief that women had no business in a man's job. I went into the job ill equipped to handle it. I did not have the physical strength at first, nor was I prepared psychologically. My skills were "culture-bound," that is, with a domestic slant. I was forced into a mode of logical and mechanical thinking and I loved it. Through further study and insights, perhaps our cultural stereotypes of male and female can be modified to accommodate women into the higher-paying skilled jobs.

The Balance of the Sexes in the Philippines

Nancy Edwards

Since 1972 when my field research ended, the Philippines has undergone two revolutions. The first, in 1972, converted Ferdinand Marcos from an elected President into a dictator through the imposition of martial law. The second, in 1986, restored democracy and replaced him with Mrs. Corazon Aquino, widow of the assassinated opposition politician, Benigno Aquino. Most female heads of state come to power through this route. They succeed to leadership of a power base built up by a husband or father. The mere fact that a woman can become head of state does not mean that the average woman in the Philippines has life chances equal to those of the average man. How are Mrs. Aquino's "sisters" faring? This question must be asked and answered by making two kinds of comparisons, that between the lives of Philippine women and Philippine men, and that between the lives of women of different cultural groups in the Philippines.

"There is a widely held assumption that in the Philippines, men and women are social equals," Jacobson (1974) states in her article "Women in Philippine Society: More Equal than Many." This judgment has been appearing in print for over sixty years. In 1919, Barton (1919: 65-69) noted that the Ifugao, a pagan people of north central Luzon, distribute property at marriage equally to the wife and husband and set equal penalties for adultery. In 1928, Kroeber (1928: 151-152), referring to peoples of the Philippines generally, described the sexes as receiving equal treatment: equality of descent from both mother and father, equality of men and women before the law under both traditional and modern law, and the lack of a rigid division of labor, i.e., men and women work cooperatively on many tasks. This assertion of sexual equality in the Philippines continues to be made (Bacdayan 1977, Green 1980).

In this paper I will try to assess the relative status of women and men in the Philippines by comparing Pagan, Christian and Muslim women and men. Except for Kroeber, these authors did not include Muslims in their comparison, perhaps because there was and is no published ethnography of a Muslim village. Using my own unpublished field data on Samal Muslim women of Mindanao, I will show that the case for equality of the sexes becomes even stronger when Muslim women are included.

First, however, let me give a brief description of the Philippine people.

The Philippine People

According to the 1970 Philippine Census, 83 percent of the Filipinos are Catholic, 3 percent are Protestant, 5 percent are Muslim, and 2 percent belong to indigenous religions. The term 'Pagan' is used in the Philippine literature to group together the followers of various indigenous religions to distinguish them from Christians or Muslims (followers of Islam). In the census enumerations, the numbers of Muslims and Pagans are probably underestimated since these groups often withhold cooperation from government-sponsored activities. If we categorize these religious groupings according to the languages they speak, all are equally indigenous; Philippine languages have not been replaced by either Spanish or English. Neither Spain nor the United States, the Philippines' two colonial masters, sent a sufficient number of colonists to the Philippines to influence the ethnic makeup of the country. In order to compare Filipino women with each other, I will consider each religious group separately. In addition I will subdivide them by rural versus urban and by socioeconomic status (rich versus poor).

Islam is believed to have been introduced into the Philippines by Arab, Chinese and Malay traders some time in the fourteenth century (Pallesen 1978:9). The Spanish introduced Catholicism when they colonized the Philippines in the 1560s. Conversion to Christianity was a priority policy for the Spanish administration and they succeeded in subduing and converting the lowland 'pagan' peoples. The Muslims resisted the Spanish, however. Unlike the Pagans, who were tribal peoples with minimal political institutions, they had their own form of state, e.g. the Sultanate of Sulu, and they had the organization and power to fight off Spanish attempts to rule or convert them. Wars and raids between the Muslims and the Catholics, sometimes initiated by one side, sometimes by the other, have continued right up to the present, only interrupted by periods of peace during American colonization from 1898 to 1942, and the Japanese Occupation from 1942 to 1945, when governmental control of the populace reached a maximum. Given this history of conflict between Catholics and Muslims, it is surprising how similar their ways of life are. The great difference at the present time is that the modern sector of the economy and most of the wealth, population and land area is in Catholic hands. Some wealthy Muslim landowners and traders exist, but the Muslim areas remain predominantly rural and unindustrialized. The lot of the poor is similar for both groups, with Christians having better access to education and thus a greater chance of advancing their economic position.

Among the Muslims there are ten ethnolinguistic groups. There are twenty Christian ethnolinguistic groups, with distinctive languages and traditions. Within the Christian population, however, the important distinctions are between rich and poor and between urban and rural. Indeed there are estimated to be between seventy and eighty different ethnic groups in the Philippines. Yet despite the diversity of language, religion, and culture among them, there are important similarities which justify viewing the Filipinos as a cultural unit (LeBar 1975:15; Fox 1963:342): all groups speak languages of the Hesperonesian Linkage of the Austronesian language family (Dyen 1965:29), and reckon descent cognaticly--that is, equally from both mother and father.

A Strategy for Comparison

With seventy to eighty different ethnic groups in the Philippines, it is impossible to make statements which apply to the situation of women in all of them. Instead I shall provide information on Philippine women in three cross-cutting categories: the religious division between Catholics, Muslims and Pagans (information on Protestant Christians is sparse so they are not included); the economic division between rich and poor; and the urban/rural division. Some of these categories have insignificant numbers of members, such as urban Pagans or rural wealthy Christians. For others, such as poor Christian women, both urban and rural, I was unable to locate information on their economic roles relative to men. They are, however, included in the social and political comparisons. Data on Muslim women come from my own fieldwork in the Zamboanga City area of Mindanao. Table 1 below shows the categories of Filipinas who are to be compared.

Table 1. Categories of Filipinas to be Compared

Urban		Rural	
Poor	Wealthy	Poor	Wealthy
Muslim	Muslim	Muslim	Muslim
Catholic	Catholic	Catholic	--------
-------	-------	Pagan	Pagan

The pagan groups chosen for comparison with the Catholics and Muslims are the Ilongot and the Bontoc Igorot, both headhunting mountain peoples of Luzon (see map in Figure 1). They contrast with the Catholics and Muslims in being not yet organized into states. While neither have elaborated political institutions, the Ilongot can be considered to have a simpler political organization than the Bontoc Igorot. Similarly the Ilongot have a "simpler" economy, shifting horticultural cultivation; the Bontoc Igorot have intensive agriculture characterized by permanent irrigation and terracing of fields.

The Ilongot were still a tribal people in 1967 when they were first visited by the Rosaldos (Rosaldo 1980a); that is, they had not submitted to the authority of the Philippine national government. In this discussion they represent the egalitarian type of Philippine political organization, characterized by little in the way of formal leadership. Authority comes from age, experience, intelligence, and personality. They are a horticultural people who grow rice by shifting cultivation. Among the Ilongot, no man holds authority over any other. Because of the respect that juniors owe their senior kinsmen, what minimal authority there is, is exercised by the oldest fathers and grandfathers who are still strong and productive.

In contrast to the shifting Ilongot, the Bontoc Igorot live in permanent settlements and plant irrigated rice in hillside terraces. In this discussion they represent a 'rank'

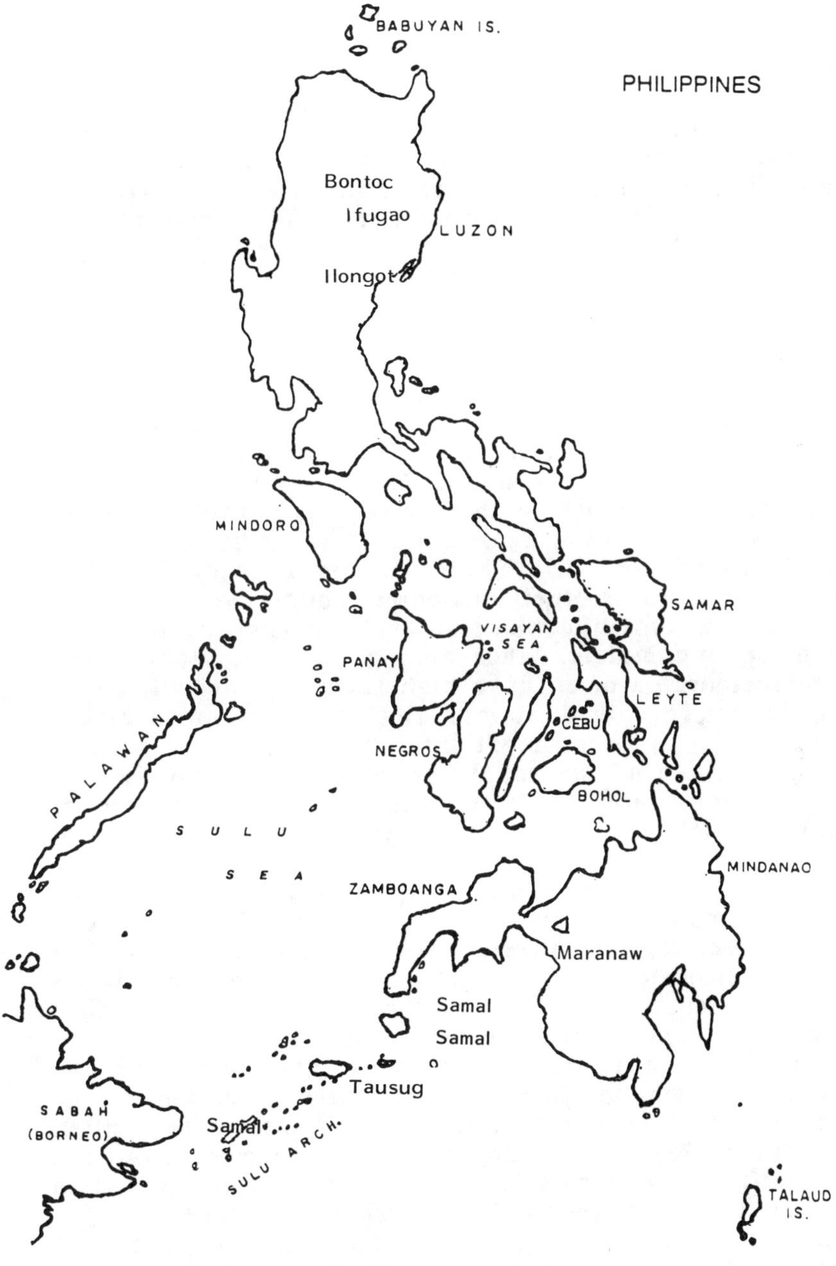
BABUYAN IS.
PHILIPPINES
Bontoc
Ifugao
LUZON
Ilongot
MINDORO
SAMAR
VISAYAN SEA
PANAY
LEYTE
CEBU
NEGROS
PALAWAN
BOHOL
SULU SEA
MINDANAO
ZAMBOANGA
Maranaw
Samal
Samal
Tausug
SABAH (BORNEO)
Samal
SULU ARCH.
TALAUD IS.

Figure 1

type of Philippine political organization. Men belong to one of three ranks, based partly upon inheritance and partly upon achievement. Women belong to their father's rank before marriage and their husband's after marriage, though the ranks usually marry endogamously. To be eligible for the highest rank, a child must be born into a high ranking landowning family, marry into one, and complete a series of expensive feastgivings. The middle rank is composed of landowning families without sufficient wealth to achieve high rank. The lowest rank is composed of landless families who work for the high-ranking families. Prior to 1902 when the American colonial government established its authority by force, each ward within a Bontoc village was governed by a council of male elders. The leaders in each council were the highest-ranking men. Also prior to 1902, a male could validate and increase his prestige through headhunting.

It is known from historical records that the ancestors of the present Christians and Muslims were once pagans with cultures similar to the egalitarian Ilongot, the more hierarchical Bontoc Igorot, or some variant of these cultures (Infante 1969). The Christianization of these two groups, as well as other Philippine mountain-dwellers, has only started to take place in the twentieth century and remains incomplete. Since among both the Ilongot and Bontoc Igorot, women have high status (as we will see in Table 2), it would appear that conversion to either Christianity or Islam might entail a decline in the relative social position of women. Historical information is lacking on this point, however, since Philippine history makers as well as history recorders, whether Spanish, American, or Filipino, have universally been male and almost universally Christian (but see Rasul 1970). A comparison of contemporary Christians, Muslims and Pagans, though indicative, cannot entirely settle a question of historical change (Rosaldo 1980b). Religious conversion has always meant submission to a Christian or Muslim state, and thus a change from tribal to peasant status. This change has so many important implications that male historians can easily lose sight of changes in the status of women. As the women's history of the Philippines comes to be written (Infante 1975), we will undoubtedly learn more about the meaning of conversion for Filipinas during the period in which the major process of conversion took place.

The Philippine people have now been introduced, as well as the specific groups to be compared. The social, economic, and political comparisons, and a summary, will follow in the next four sections. The final section considers the future of sexual equality in the Philippines.

The Social Comparison

Table 2 compares men's and women's places in the social and religious structure for Catholics and Muslims. The Catholic data combine data on the Tagalog of Luzon (Jocano 1969), the Waray of the Bisayas (Nurge 1965), the Ilocano of Luzon (M. Szanton 1972) and twenty of the largest Christian groups covered by Hart (Hart 1975:16-22). The Muslim data come from my observations of the Muslim Samal of the Zamboanga City area. I have noted differences between Muslim groups, where I know of them. The categories represented in the table were chosen from three partially overlapping sets of categories:

1) the most basic categories of social organization, e.g. descent;

2) categories in which men receive preferential treatment in many non-Philippine societies, e.g. modern education; and

3) categories where practices differ from what might be expected, e.g. neither unmarried nor married Filipina Muslim women are secluded from the gaze of men.

On the basis of these comparisons, the situation of Christian and Muslim women is very similar. The disabilities which Middle Eastern Islam places on women have apparently never been part of Philippine Islam. A comparison of Christians and Muslims with groups still practicing traditional Philippine religions can give us some idea of the effect which religious conversion has had on the status of women.

Both Islam and Christianity are male-centered religions. Adoption of these religions could have resulted in a major decline in women's status. But comparison shows only a slight decline as a consequence of putting a value on virginity for unmarried women. Differences in courtship between Christians and Muslims on the one hand and the Bontoc Igorot and the Ilongot on the other may be related to conversion.

Philippine pagan customs are not as familiar as those of Christians and Muslims so they require a more complete description than is possible in a table. Traditionally, unmarried Bontoc women slept together in a girls' dormitory. Their suitors spent the nights with them there. The men spent the days working for their prospective in-laws. When pregnancy ensued, the couple was officially married with a ceremony (Lebar 1975:82-86). Ilongot

Table 2. Comparison of Male and Female Participation in Social Life for Philippine Christians and Muslims

Area of Comparison	Christian (Catholic)	Muslim
1. Type of descent	Cognatic (not favoring either the mother's or the father's side at the expense of the other)	Cognatic
2. Inheritance	Equal inheritance to sons and daughters	Equal inheritance. Do not follow Islamic law of double portion of inheritance to sons.
3. Marriage, impact on status of legal majority	Teenagers become full adults. Avoidance of marriage possible.	Both men and women must marry to achieve full adulthood. The few never-married adults are explained as the result of spells cast by disappointed suitors.
4. Choice of partner	Marriages sometimes arranged for the children of wealthy parents. Otherwise the choice made by the parties with parental advice. Elopement possible if parents object. No positive marriage rule.	Same.
5. Residence	With husband's or wife's parents early in marriage, depending on the wishes of all parties. Independent when the couple can afford their own house.	With husband's or wife's parents or alternating between both sets of parents, depending on the wishes of all parties. Independent when the couple can afford their own house.
6. Child care	Women have overall responsibility. Older children and men also can do all child care tasks except nursing. Fathers enjoy caring for their children.	Same
7. Female sexual conduct before marriage	Virginity at marriage expected. When boys and girls meet, the girls are chaperoned.	Wealthy families may restrict their daughters. Others allow them sexual freedom if the youths conceal their activities from anyone who might make the matter public.

8. Female sexual conduct after marriage	No sex partner other than the husband allowed.	Same.
9. Male sexual conduct before and after marriage	Expected to seek intercourse with all unmarried women.	Same.*
10. Polygyny (multiple wives)	Absent, but taking of mistresses condoned if concealed from the wife.	Present but not common. First wives often initiate a divorce if the husband marries a second time.
11. Female seclusion or veiling	Absent	Absent**
12. Divorce	Absent	Both men and women can initiate divorce but men can do so more easily.
13. Remarriage after divorce or death of spouse	Encouraged if there are still young children. Otherwise optional.	Same.
14. Religious office	Only males can be priests. Females can be nuns.	Only men can hold positions as mosque officers. Older women and men can be religious teachers and pilgrims to Mecca.
15. Modern education	Considered appropriate for both sexes. More girls than boys attend college and graduate school.	Education not as highly valued nor as accessible as to Christians. More boys than girls attend school and college.
16. Warfare	Traditionally men were the warriors. Women did not fight. They appear as casualties. Women currently serve in the Armed Forces of the Philippines in non-combatant roles.	Same.

*The Tausug and Samal discourage the sexual activity of both men and women outside of marriage. Transgressions are not important, however, unless the couple is seen or the woman reveals the incident. If it becomes known that a man has even touched a woman not his wife, he must pay a fine. The woman is not punished (Keifer 1872:37). The goal here is more to preserve the family than to preserve virginity. If an unmarried girl does become pregnant, her word is accepted as to the identity of the father and they must marry, even if it is a second marriage for the husband. Thus "illegitimate" children cannot be born. The husband can divorce her right after the birth if he wishes.

**Women of the Maranaw are restricted to the household and do no work or even shop outside the home (Fox 1963).

courtship was similar except that it took place at the girl's home. The suitor worked for the girl's parents. If he found favor with her and with them, he would be allowed to sleep with her. However, until the marriage was confirmed by a ceremony, he might still be rejected. For neither group was the loss of a woman's virginity before marriage a cause for concern.

The introduction of the idea of preserving female virginity until marriage means that adolescent women must be guarded. The Muslim means of control is usually to keep adolescent women at home. Thus they do not get the opportunities for education and travel that adolescent boys do. Christian adolescent women have presumably internalized a bar to sexual intimacy before marriage. They are allowed to attend school with boys. The girls' peer group is always present to prevent the opportunity for private contact between the sexes. This means of enforcing the double standard is a minor handicap, if at all, to a woman's social and intellectual development. Unmarried Christian women can even sometimes emigrate to the United States with parental encouragement.

A comparison of religious specialists shows that women did not hold these positions within either pagan group. The Ilongot have no religious specialists. The practice of shamanism by males has died out, leaving each woman and man to seek magical aid individually. Women seek aid from a female spirit and men from a male spirit. All Bontoc religious specialists are male, though lay women can conduct some ceremonies. Since the direction of bias is the same in Christianity and Islam, women cannot be said to have lost ground in the specifically religious sphere.

With regard to divorce, it is possible but rare for both the Bontoc and the Ilongot. The loss of the option of divorce is more of a hindrance for Christian women than it is for men, since men can take mistresses. Poor Christians can take the option of unofficial "divorce" in which the spouses simply part company and seek other "unofficial spouses."

When the remaining twelve comparisons are extended to the two pagan groups, we see three outcomes. The pagans are similar to the Muslims and Christians in the areas of descent, female sexual conduct after marriage, and female seclusion. In the case of polygyny, the Bontoc allow it while the Ilongot do not. In the case of inheritance and residence, the pagans behave differently from either the Muslims or the Christians but the difference is neither to the advantage nor to the disadvantage of women. For the Ilongot, "land traditionally belongs to those who clear it. . . . other property is individually held and rarely inherited" (Lebar 1975:104). According to Rosaldo (1980a), residence is with the wife's family. The husband clears the land with the aid of his in-laws, but the wife grows the crops and controls the distribution of the food she produces. A field is abandoned after three years, at which point 'ownership' becomes moot. For the Bontoc the best field and the largest share of other property goes to the oldest child, whether male or female. Inheritance is at a child's marriage rather than upon the death of the parents (Lebar 1975:84).

The highly important factor of residence, which for the Ilongots is with the wife's family, is unclear for the Bontoc Igorot. LeBar (1975:84) notes:

> Jenks (1905:69) suggests neolocal, with the girl's father providing the house; whereas Keesing (1949:568) says that the house is customarily provided by the groom's family and that residence is primarily patrilocal.

Information was not available for Ilongot or Bontoc for the remaining categories. In no case where information is available do the two pagan groups treat women less equally than do the Muslims or the Catholics.

The Economic Comparison

The smallest cohesive unit of Philippine social, economic and political life is the married couple with children. This is true for both Muslims and Christians, even though Muslims have divorce and Christians do not. Most Muslim divorces occur early in marriage when there are few children or none at all.

All sibling ties remain important in adult life, the more so if the siblings continue to live near each other. Kin ties affect, but do not determine, the composition of organized groups. Adult children continue to follow the advice of their parents until they marry or move out of the parental home. Married children manage their own economic affairs, even if they live with their parents. If they do, parents and children buy and cook their food cooperatively but they do not pool the rest of their resources since they usually plan to live together only temporarily. In practice, the degree of parental influence on adult children depends on the age and wealth of the parents. Poor and aged parents become the dependents of their children and lose most of their influence. Wealthy parents can control their adult children more easily by using the threat of withdrawal of support.

Each newly-married couple represents the embryo of a "family firm." The husband assures its present survival by bringing in the primary income. A woman's obligation is first to childbearing and second to income production. The wife assures the ultimate survival of the family by producing children to support herself and her husband in their old age. In the rural Philippines, whether we refer to Christians or to Muslims, the ideal number of children is the maximum number compatible with the mother's health and the children's survival. The completed rural family size is often as many as seven living children in areas with poor medical facilities, and ten or more where medical facilities are good.

In urban areas wealthy couples may use contraceptives in order to space children, but they often still have large numbers of children. Middle class families may plan to limit the size of their families if three conditions can be met:

1. The cost of childrearing becomes a problem. Housing and food cost more in the city. Education, considered necessary for a child through high school and perhaps even college, may be a heavy expense;
2. Good environmental sanitation and medical care insure the survival of the children a couple already has; a couple need not have many children in order to insure that a few survive; and
3. The parents can accumulate enough wealth through investments to be able to support themselves in retirement, so they are less dependent upon the support of their children. (The Philippines has no Social Security system.)

While all families in the city find necessities to be expensive (condition 1 above), it is poor families that may suffer from poor sanitation and inadequate medical care (condition 2) and be unable to save for their old age (condition 3), so it is the poor that have large families, even in the cities. In general, Filipinos see children as both necessary and desirable (Bulatao 1975:10). Even couples who want small families rarely want fewer than four children, two of each sex.

The way in which a woman balances her obligations to bear and rear children and to do other productive work for the family firm depends on many circumstances: her own, her husband's and her children's. Women do productive labor in all the indigenous Philippine groups, so it seems likely that the idea of the home-staying, non-working wife must have been introduced from outside by the Spanish or the Americans. There are some husbands in the middle and upper levels who prefer that their wives not work. Otherwise, a married woman is always considered to be a potential worker, but she must suit her actual participation in income production to her own and her family's life cycle.

The information cited below on Christian women workers comes from Castillo and Guerrero (1966; see also Rosenzweig 1976), and concerns middle and upper income women. There are many fewer middle to upper income Muslims as compared to Catholics, and information on the work life of Muslim women in this social segment is not readily available. The information about Muslim women which I do have comes from my own research among poor Muslim Samal women of the Zamboanga City area of Mindanao.

Among middle and upper income Christian women, those most likely to work are those with a college education or better, who can command a good salary. These women have from one to three maids who do their cooking, laundry, housecleaning, and child care. They are still not free of home responsibilities, however; they continue to do most of the infant care at night, marketing and general family service, as for example, sewing on buttons. Castillo and Guerrero do not mention the amount of family service performed by husbands.

In Sylvia Guerrero's survey, when women were asked if they would quit working if their husbands asked them to, 44 percent said yes, 39 percent said no, and 17 percent said, "It depends on the reason but it had better be a good one." Among those who said "yes," the majority gave as the reason, "He is the boss." This shows acceptance of the husband as the more significant decision-maker by something less than 50 percent of these highly educated women.

It is not necessarily the case, however, that highly educated women should uniformly want to possess, or actually possess, equal decisionmaking power with their husbands. These are the women most heavily exposed through their education to European and American stereotypes of male/female inequality as well as equality. The specifically Spanish influence is not conspicuous considering that Spain held the Philippines from the 1560s until 1898 when the Americans took over. For example, Spanish is no longer spoken except in the homes of a few "old families" who first became prominent during the Spanish colonial period. Catholicism was Spain's most significant contribution to the Philippines.

The Spanish also provided some education for women starting in 1574 (Arceo-Ortega 1963). They began public education for both sexes in 1863, and the Americans continued it. The positive contribution of modern education is that it gives women access to the modern economy. At present women outnumber men in education, pharmacy and dentistry. If present trends in graduate study continue, women will soon outnumber men in medicine, law, accounting, and engineering (Green 1980). Many women engage in business, both as owners and managers, though they are not found among the managers of the largest corporations.

One possible reason for the acceptance of the husband as "the boss" in many wealthier families is the marriage of Filipina women with Chinese men, which occurs frequently in this social stratum. Chinese men have been immigrating to the Philippines for at least the last 400 years. They engage in commerce and marry and live with Filipinas. If they convert to Catholicism, by the second generation they are accepted as Filipino. If they have prospered in business, they are accepted by other wealthy Filipinos, many of whom have Chinese ancestors themselves (Wickberg 1965). When a Chinese man and a Filipina marry, the children are brought up to reckon descent from both parents and to speak a Philippine language. But they may also speak Chinese and know something of patrilineal descent and the deference accorded to males in the Chinese system. The overall effect of many generations of intermarriage has probably been to raise male status relative to females within wealthier Filipino families.

Since anthropologists are rarely able to do field research among wealthy members of any culture, we are often forced to turn to other sources of information. A novel published in 1968, *Like the Wind I Go,* by Liesel Quirino, depicts the rise of a Filipina businesswoman, daughter of a German man and a Filipina, from poverty to great wealth. She begins her business career just after the liberation of the Philippines from the Japanese, an ideal time to be an upstart. She starts with an embroidery business employing other women to do the embroidery which she sells at great profit to the Americans. She has obtained her initial capital by marrying a divorced but wealthy doctor; he subsequently takes no further part in her ventures. The profit from the embroidery business she invests in an office building which she rents out. She goes on from that to even larger enterprises. Her path to riches through ever larger business dealings is the same as the one explained to us by men in the Muslim village we studied in the Zamboanga area. Her success is attributed to her skill, and she never meets with opposition from men on the basis of her sex. She meets with discrimination, not because she is a woman, but because she is half German. All the subordinates in her corporation are men, including her younger brother. Her motivation both to marry a divorced man whom she did not love, and to work so hard, is to save her family from poverty. While it is a kind of female Horatio Alger story, it nevertheless shows what is conceived as realistic for a Filipina to do.

My information on poor women concerns specifically poor Muslim Samal women in rural and urban areas. Women usually start working as adolescents, depending upon opportunity and inclination. The following sketch is of an actual rural woman as she was in 1980: Sabtura is an adolescent girl living with her parents and her brothers on an island off the Zamboanga Peninsula. She has certain duties assigned to her on account of her age and sex, such as doing the daily family washing, and she takes turns with her mother doing the cooking. In fact, everyone in her family, even her nine-year-old brother, knows how to cook, but she and her mother are the ones who do it because it is a duty of women. Since Sabtura has no very young brothers and sisters, she need not do childcare. When her regular duties are done, she helps her mother do whatever she asks her to do. But when her mother doesn't need help, she is free to do what she wants. She chooses to spend some time gossiping with maidens of her own age, but she doesn't spend all her time that way. She is an industrious girl and a member of a poor family. She knows that her family can't afford to give her as many new clothes as she would like to have to catch the eye of the village boys and eventually attract a husband. Therefore she makes snacks to sell to her fellow villagers. The money she gets she divides between helping her father to put a new roof on the house and buying clothes for herself. She wishes to attract the notice of unmarried men so that she can choose her husband from among several possibilities when she is ready to marry. An adolescent boy, her brother for example, is nearly as capable a fisherman as his father and can earn much more money than she can, both for his family and for himself.[1] He needs the money because he must amass a substantial sum to pay to the parents of his bride-to-be to regularize his marriage, even when he marries by elopement.

Girls have more varied ways of earning money (see Table 3), but all of them are far less remunerative. In rural areas unmarried women work as often as married women. Married women employ all the same moneymaking strategies plus weaving pandanus mats and, in the early 1970s at least, investing in inter-island trading. However, men invest in inter-island trade much more often than women do because they have more money to invest.

In urban areas, money making opportunities for both men and women are greater, but the economy is divided into Christian and Muslim sectors. By the Muslim sector I mean shops which: 1) deal in traditional Muslim goods such as cloth imported from Malaysia; 2) deal in fish--fishermen in the Zamboanga area are all Muslim; or 3) serve a Muslim clientele. Women run these shops either independently or along with their husbands.

Table 3. Occupations of Unmarried Women in a Rural Village near Zamboanga

Types	Examples
Making snacks for local sale	Local versions of pancakes, donuts and other sweets composed mainly of various starches and sugar.
Animal raising and marketing	Ducks, chickens and goats.
Trading	Cloth piece goods or minor household supplies.
Working in the family business	Only two families had businesses (general stores) in 1972.

After marriage a woman in a rural area, either Christian or Muslim, usually stops working and turns the obligation of her support over to her husband. She is ready to start having children and usually has several, one right after the other. She will return to work when she has the time, or when forced by necessity. The older a wife becomes, the more time she is likely to spend working and the less time on childrearing. Even if she is still bearing children, they can be taken care of much of the time by the older children.

Overall, rural women's occupations do not produce a good profit. The occupation with the greatest potential for profit is trading. The highest-earning women ever to visit one village near Zamboaga was a married produce trader who lived on a nearby island and brought occasional boatloads of cassava (also called manioc), bananas and fruit to sell. She came in a chartered boat by herself, sold her produce, stayed overnight in the village, and was picked up again the next day. Her unusual behavior was explained as, "She wants to make the pilgrimage to Mecca." This pilgrimage is a religious obligation for all Muslims who can afford it. But since the Philippines is on the other side of the globe from Mecca, the cost is such that only better-off families would think of trying to accumulate the money.[2] In urban areas women have the potential to support themselves and their families. In at least one case, a Muslim woman schoolteacher worked while her husband stayed home and looked after their two children.

While Christians and Muslims participate in the Philippine national economy, the Bontoc and the Ilongot still provide most of their own subsistence. Bontoc women and men help each other to grow rice and other crops with a minimal division of labor. The Ilongot economy is marked by a definite division of labor: women grow rice and men hunt.

The following composite sketch of an adolescent girl is built up from Rosaldo (1980a) and relates to the period before 1972: Sili lives in a small settlement in the mountain forests of Nueva Viscaya with her parents and brothers and sisters. She is a 'true maiden,' as the Ilongot say, old enough to do the same work her mother does but not yet married. In addition to working in her family's home and in her mother's fields she can travel to the households of distant kin to spend a while aiding them. She works hard but there is pleasure for her in that she meets her peers, both male and female, whom she would not meet if she stayed at home in her own small settlement. She cannot travel as her male age mates do, in a peer group. It is too dangerous, since a group of women might meet a headhunting party on the trail. In their travels, males sometimes work for "outsiders" and earn money, but she will not have this chance. She waits to see who will come courting her. A suitor must satisfy her and her family, especially her brothers, since the couple are going to live with her family for some time after marriage. After marriage she will begin to farm on her own account. Men will clear the forest for her swidden field, but then she performs the rest of the work. The food she produces belongs to her, and she gains prestige from a large harvest. The grain is hers to give or withhold. If her co-resident kin are not satisfied with her generosity when they are in need of food, they may move away. If they do, they break up her husband's political alliances. By supplying food, a woman cements alliances, even though she cannot speak in men's formal political councils.

In summary, women's economic participation is limited by all the same factors that limit men's economic participation: investment capital available, education, imagination, etc. Their role as childbearers and child-rearers is an additional limitation. It is a practical limitation, however, and is not applied to women who do not have children or who are able to make other arrangements for child care. None of the Philippine religious ideologies examined above defines women as incapable in the economic sphere.

The Political Comparison

For both rich and poor, Muslim and Christian, the "official representative" of the family to the outside world is the husband. The wife can represent the family in contexts in which she is known to be trusted by her husband to do so, such as in the family business. Within the family, the woman holds the family purse (Castillo and Guerrero 1966). The husband cannot make decisions which involve spending money without getting the wife's concurrence. The degree to which she takes part in the actual decisionmaking process depends on the degree to which she will be involved in the implementation of the decision; for example, the husband decides which farm implements to buy, while the wife decides on household furnishings.

To get some idea as to why the husband represents the family in the political and legal context today, we need to look at what may have been going on before the Spanish and American colonizations of the Philippines altered the situation. Men appear to dominate in these contexts because they know how to use weapons to defend their families and attack others. In the state of perpetual petty warfare which seems to have existed before the introduction of the state by Spanish and Muslim rulers, war, politics and the legal system were fused. He who wanted his legal rights respected had to have might on his side, whether individually or in a politically-organized group. Women scarcely appeared in this arena unless the men were disputing about them.

The best information we have on this question--why men rather than women ideally represent the group to the outside world--comes from Rosaldo's 1980a study of the Ilongot people of central Luzon. According to records, these people took their last head in 1972 and are now being converted to Christianity. Among men, there is no principle of authority recognized except relative age. Nevertheless, husbands can command their wives. Women defer to their husbands because they say, "They are stronger . . . wiser . . . and angrier, . . . and because they have killed their fellow human beings" (Rosaldo 1980a:99-100). Men's authority cannot be based on their defense of their family, at least not in the usual sense. This is because the purpose of most attacks is to take heads and the attacks are made by stealth. With surprise on their side, the raiders are almost always successful in killing the individual or small group who are their chosen victims. It is sometimes weeks or months before the bereaved kinsmen can find out who the killers were. The mounting of an immediate revenge raid is not common.

The Ilongot have rather poor dispute settlement mechanisms. In-group cohesion is maintained by hostility to out-groups, and this is expressed through headhunting. A couple lives at the wife's place, and whenever a new marriage is to be arranged, it is with these same groups with whom there is hostility. Hence even the arrangement of marriages cannot take place easily; some relative of the proposed groom must pay a fine for past killings of members of the bride's group. War, politics and the legal system thus shade into one another. In the legal system only men are the official speakers and only men claim damages. Men are all equals; none has authority over any other. The right to collect damages rests on male willingness to fight if they do not receive what they regard as their due.

Though brought up in a manner similar to her brothers and able to perform almost all the same subsistence tasks, even hunting--women hunt when men are absent, or they help men hunt--the Ilongot woman submits to the command of her husband. In return he does his best to protect her from a violent death by making sure that everyone knows of his readiness to inflict it. His usual proof of this is to take at least one head from a member of an enemy group.

Turning to the Western Bontoc of northern Luzon we see a group which abandoned headhunting at the turn of the century. Albert S. Bacdayan, in his 1977 article, has alleged that this group treats men and women equally. Bacdayan is particularly qualified to speak about this group because he himself is a member of it.

In his view the most important reason why men and women are equal is the interchangeability of tasks between men and women and the many tasks on which men and women cooperate; that is, the sexual division of labor is minimal. The information in Table 4 was gathered by interview and observation in two villages. It was coded as performed by males only (M), performed by females only (F), performed equally by males or females (B), performed usually by males (MF), and performed usually by females (FM).

Table 4. Tasks and Their Performers in Tanulong and Fedilizan (Bacdayan 1977)[3]

Task	Performer
Agricultural or Subsistence Tasks	
Preparation of the soil	B
Planting	B
Weeding the banks of the fields	B
Plowing with animals (usually carabao)	M
Weeding in between rice plants	FM
Watering	B
Erecting scarecrows	MF
Guarding against rice birds	B
Trapping rats and mice	M
Installing magical objects to scare rats	B
Checking to see if rice is ready for harvest	B
Harvesting	B
Sowing seeds	F
Removing seedlings from seedbeds	B
Clearing upland fields	MF
Planting vegetables	B

Clearing the padi dikes	FM
Fertilizing with organic matter, usually cut grass	B
Planting beans	FM
Weeding upland sweet potato fields	FM
Fencing	B
Building stone/earth walls	MF
Fixing dikes	B
Fertilizing with mineral soil	B
Planting sweet potato vines	FM
Digging up sweet potatoes	FM
Preparing upland fields	B
Taking care of animals in the pasture	MF
Cutting grass for animals	MF
Cutting sticks for fencing and poles	B
Preparing bamboo for binding rice bundles	MF
Milling sugar cane	B
Hauling rice from the fields	MF
Digging up new upland fields	B
House-building Tasks	
Gathering thatch roofing	B
Roofing	M
Gathering vines for binding	M
Preparing wood	M
Preparing the ground for building	B
Hauling the material to building site	B
Religious Functions	
Saying prayers	B
Performing sacrifices	B
Calling for souls and spirits	B
Being mediums	B
Performing sacrifices to the sacred tree	M
Ritual first planting	F
Ritual observing of omen birds outside the village in a mock headhunting expedition	M
Ritual counteraction of bad spirits	M
Domestic Household Chores	
Cooking	B
Washing dishes	B
Feeding animals	B
Skinning sweet potatoes	FM
Pounding rice	B
Keeping floors clean	FM
Gathering sweet potatoes for pigs	FM

Waking up to cook in the morning	B
Splitting wood	MF
Cutting wood from the forest	MF
Preparing pig's food for cooking	B
Preparing cotton thread for weaving	FM
Weaving cloth	F
Washing clothes	FM
Sewing/mending clothes	FM
Washing dishes and pans	FM
Dressing and sacrificing chickens	B
Killing pigs	M
Distributing meat	MF
Cutting up meat for meals	MF
Fetching water	B
Babysitting	B
Keeping the child clean	FM
Feeding the child	B
Washing the child	FM
Cutting child's hair	MF
Seeing the medium when child is sick	B
Taking care of sick child	FM
Counseling children	B
Search for Food	
Fishing in the river	MF
Trapping birds	M
Gathering mushrooms	M
Snaring rice birds	M
Trapping fish in the rice fields	MF
Gathering edible snails	FM
Gathering beetles	B
Hunting	M

The most striking thing about these tables is how equally the agricultural and domestic tasks are divided. Neither men nor women seem to specialize in either the dirty or the boring tasks.

There is one sphere in which Bacdayan admits that there is inequality between men and women. Men dominate in the formal political arena and hold all the elective offices. He attributes this to the previously-practiced tradition of headhunting in which men were both the attackers and the defenders while women could only participate as victims. The significant point he makes is that now that women are beginning to run for public office (they have yet to run successfully), they do not encounter opposition purely on account of their sex. However, the threat of violence is still used as a political weapon. When groups of men from two villages, Tanowong (Tanulong) and Agawa, met to discuss an irrigation dispute, for example, threats to resort to force were made by both sides (Bacdayan 1974).

The situation for women in the Philippines varies from one cultural group to another, and the situation for all women is in flux. Contemporary Christian and Muslim women have increasing opportunities for participation in the modern economy which Pagan women rarely enjoy unless they convert to one or the other religion. Access to the professions through education has meant a greater representation of women in the professions, exceeding 50 percent in some cases. In politics also there has been the equalizing factor of suffrage for women in the Philippine Republic, so that the potential exists for equal participation of men and women in the political arena. The overall direction of change for Philippine women has yet to make itself clear. At present, however, women probably come closer to equality in the Philippines than anywhere else in the modern world.

The Future of Sexual Equality in the Philippines

Jo Freeman has formulated three principles of sexist thought:

> 1. Men do the important work in the world and the work done by men is what is important.
> 2. Women are here for the pleasure and assistance of men, and
> 3. Women's identities are defined by their relationship to men and their social value is determined by that of the men they are related to.
>
> (Freeman 1972:211-212)

We anthropologists make a search for societies where men and women are more equal in order to discover what changes we need to make in our own society in order for women to achieve equality. There are two schools of thought on what changes in women's activities would raise their status. One is Bacdayan's position: if men and women are equal owners and equal workers, they will become equal in other respects as well. This is the impetus behind the Equal Rights Amendment. The other school of thought says that women need not change their activities. Men's and women's work can be equally valued and valuable even though they perform different tasks.

However, this seems unlikely. Just why Ilongot men and women should value men's headhunting and hunting more than women's rice-growing and baby production is not obvious to the outsider. Both tasks are necessary to the survival of the group, the women's possibly more so than the men's. It would seem to be a clear case of Sexist Principle #1: "Men do the important work . . ."

Does the establishment of a monopoly of force by the Philippine state mean that women can now achieve full political equality?[4] Are women moving toward equality or away from it? The chief threat to fuller equality appears to be the values of outside cultures, aspects of which the Filipinos may be adopting through modern education; I have already mentioned the probable decline in status for women in the acceptance of male-centered religions like Islam and Catholic Christianity, and the acceptance of traits from male-dominated cultures like the Chinese. Other aspects of Euroamerican androcentrism may well be absorbed along with Western-style education.

In the face of these countertrends, equality in education and the state monopoly of force may not be sufficient to bring about sexual equality. Indeed Filipina women could lose their lead and slip to the level of European and American women.

Notes

Acknowledgements. I wish to thank the Samal people of both island and mainland southwestern Mindanao for their cooperation as well as the National Science Foundation grant GS 30526 for supporting field research in the area from August 1971 to September 1972. Thanks also to Michelle Rosaldo who first pointed out to me the significance of this topic and to Robert Randall for reading and commenting on earlier drafts.

1. Adolescent girls are allowed to fish also, but sexual distance rules limit the men with whom they may share a boat. Girls may fish with their brothers but not with their fathers or other males. This rule makes it hard for

an unmarried girl to learn to fish. After marriage, a woman's boat companion would be her husband.

2. Usually the husband goes to Mecca first. If there is money enough to send the wife as well, she goes later, probably after passing the age of menopause. It is not thought proper to send unmarried young people to Mecca since, with so much of their lives ahead of them, they would probably not be able to fulfill the obligation pilgrims incur to live the rest of their lives righteously.

3. Permission to reprint this table has been granted by Columbia University Press.

4. The Philippine government monopoly of force in the Bontoc region is not firmly established even yet. On September 13, 1986, Corazon Aquino accepted the surrender of an Igorot rebel army which had taken up arms to oppose the Marcos government's attempt to dam the Chico River. In return she promised to cancel the dam.

References Cited

Arceo-Ortega, Angelina
1963 A Career-Housewife in the Philippines. *In* Women in the New Asia: The Changing Social Roles of Men and Women in South and Southeast Asia. Barbara Ward, ed. pp. 365-373. Paris: UNESCO.

Bacdayan, Albert S.
1974 Securing Water for Drying Rice Terraces: Irrigation, Community Organization and Expanding Social Relationships in a Western Bontoc Group, Philippines. Ethnology 13:247-260.

1977 Mechanistic Cooperation and Sexual Equality Among the Western Bontoc. *In* Sexual Stratification: A Cross-Cultural View. Alice Schlegel, ed. pp. 270-291. Copyright © 1977 Columbia University Press. By permission.

Barton, Roy F.
1969 Ifugao Law. University of California Publications in American Archaeology and Ethnology, Vol. 15, No. 1 (1st ed. 1919).

Bulatao, Rodolfo A.
1975 The Value of Children: A Cross-National Study. Vol. II, Philippines. East West Center, Honolulu: University Press of Hawaii.

Castillo, Gelia T., and Sylvia Guerrero
1966 The Filipina Woman: A Study in Multiple Roles. Journal of Asian and African Studies 1:18-29.

Draper, Patricia
1975 !Kung Women: Contrast in Sexual Egalitarianism in Foraging and Sedentary Contexts: *In* Toward an Anthropology of Women. Rayna Reiter, ed. pp. 77-109. New York: Monthly Review Press.

Dyen, Isadore
1965 A Lexico-Statistical Classification of Austronesian Languages. Indiana University Publications in Anthropology and Linguistics, Memoir 19.

Estioko-Griffin, Agnes and P. Bion Griffin
1981 Woman the Hunter: The Agta. *In* Woman the Gatherer. Frances Dahlberg, ed. pp. 121-151. New Haven: Yale University Press.

Fox, Robert
1963 Men and Women in the Philippines. *In* Women in the New Asia: The Changing Social Roles of Men and Women in South and Southeast Asia. Barbara Ward, ed. pp. 342-364. Paris: UNESCO.

Freeman, Jo
1972 The Women's Liberation Movement. *In* Marriage, Family and the Struggle of the Sexes. H. P. Dreitzel, ed. pp. 201-216. New York: Macmillan Co.

Green, Justin
1980 Are Filipinas "More Equal" than Western Women? Asia. Nov/Dec 35:37-44.

Hart, Donn V.
1975 Christian Filipinos. *In* Ethnic Groups of Insular Southeast Asia. Vol. II, Philippines and Formosa. Frank Lebar, ed. pp. 16-22. New Haven: Human Relations Area File Press.

Infante, Teresita R.
1975 The Woman in the Early Philippines and Among the Cultural Minorities. Manila: University of Santo Tomas Press.

Jacobson, Helga E.
1974 Women in Philippine Society: More Equal than Many. *In* Many Sisters: Women in Cross Cultural Perspective. Carolyn J. Mathiasson, ed. pp. 349-377. Glencoe, Ill.: Free Press.

Jenks, Albert E.
1905 The Bontoc Igorot. Washington, DC: Department of the Interior, Ethnological Survey Publications No. 1:1-266.

Jocano, F. Landa
1969 Growing Up in a Philippine Barrio. New York: Holt, Rinehart and Winston.

Keesing, Felix M.
1949 Some Notes on Bontoc Social Organization, Northern Philippines. American Anthropologist 51:578-601.

Kiefer, Thomas M.
1972 The Tausug: Violence and Law in the Philippine Moslem Society. New York: Holt, Rinehart and Winston. 1986 reissued by Waveland Press, Inc.

Kroeber, Alfred L.
1973 Peoples of the Philippines. Westport, Conn.: Greenwood Press (first edition, American Museum of Natural History Handbook Series No. 8, 1928).

Lebar, Frank M., ed.
1975 Ethnic Groups of Insular Southeast Asia. Vol. II, Philippines and Formosa. New Haven: Human Relations Area File Press.

Mydans, Seth
1986 Aquino in Truce with 100 Tribal Rebels, New York Times, Sept. 14, p. 3.

Nurge, Ethel
1965 Life in a Leyte Village. Seattle: University of Washington Press.

Pallesen, A. Kemp
1978 Culture Contact and Language Convergence. Ph.D. dissertation, Anthropology Department, University of California at Berkeley.

Quirino, Liesel Commans
1968 Like the Wind I Go. Manila: R. P. Garcia Publishing Company.

Rasul, Jainal D.
1970 The Philippine Muslims: Struggle for Identity. Manila: Nueva Era Press.

Rosaldo, Michelle Z.
1980a Knowledge and Passion: Ilongot Notions of Self and Social Life. Cambridge University Press.

1980b The Use and Abuse of Anthropology: Reflections on Feminism and Cross-cultural Understanding. Signs: Journal of Women in Culture and Society 5(3):389-417.

Rosenzweig, Mark R.
1976 Female Work Experience, Employment Status and Birth Expectations: Sequential Decisionmaking in the Philippines. Demography 13:339-356.

Szanton, Maria Christina
1972 A Right to Survive: Subsistence Marketing in a Lowland Philippine Town. University Park: Pennsylvania State University Press.

Vreeland, Nena, et al.
1976 Area Handbook for the Philippines. Washington, D.C.: U.S. Government Printing Office.

Wickberg, Edgar
1965 The Chinese in Philippine Life 1850-1898. New Haven: Yale University Press.

Sex Roles: The Position and Consciousness of Women and Men in West Germany

Helge Pross

Throughout Western Europe, the basic pattern in the social relationship between men and women is similar; all countries are dominated economically and politically by men. Men make and administer the laws, hold government offices, control corporations, political parties, the mass media, the universities, the churches, and the military. Not only positions of power, but also the qualified professions are occupied predominantly by men, whether doctors or lawyers, engineers or civil servants, professors, senior white-collar or skilled workers. Nowadays, of course, almost everywhere, a few highly-qualified women occupy middle and upper positions in the hierarchies of power, but in most countries, their numbers are still so small that one can hardly speak of a change in the basic pattern. Women do the housework, look after the children, do the jobs of subordinate status, or, alternatively, the jobs close to their work in the family: in education, nursing or service. In broad outline, this is the same distribution of function and status between the sexes that existed twenty years ago.

This essential uniformity taken into account, closer scrutiny reveals differences *between* the various Western European countries; and despite the persistence of the basic pattern over time, these are notable differences between earlier times and the present. Everywhere changes are in evidence. In this paper, a few of these changes, as exemplified in West Germany, will be outlined with occasional references to corresponding developments in other Western European countries, as well as comparison with the Soviet Union and other socialist countries. Because changes in the *relationship* between the sexes have been predominantly due to changes in the *situation* for women, I shall deal with women's situation in greater detail than men's.

First, the legal position. In West Germany, men and women have fully equal legal rights. The only distinctions involve special pregnancy and maternity regulations and a few older, protective regulations such as the prohibition on night work for women in factories. There is no longer any *systematic* discrimination against women in German law. The view that women should be treated by legislatures or courts as legally inferior no longer has any advocates. Equal rights have at last been achieved, an essential requisite for a more far-reaching conception of sexual equality: men and women participating on equal terms in *all* spheres of life which involve both sexes, and equality of opportunity for personal development.

As for putting this far-reaching conception into practice, West Germany clearly has a long way to go, as becomes clear when one studies the relationship between men and women in work, family, and politics.

Women at Work

Women have long been established in employment outside the home; almost 40 percent of the total work force in West Germany are women, in all just less than ten million. But women have not been integrated into the work force on equal terms with men. The overwhelming majority work on the lower rungs of the company ladder. Only about 10 percent of female manual workers are skilled, and scarcely more than 20 percent of non-manual women workers have attained middle or upper positions. This latter group, which includes teachers, secretaries, nurses and academic assistants in private industry, forms the peak of the working females' population pyramid. Almost all of these highly-placed women are under the authority of male supervisors and managers (Pross 1973). In the highly-esteemed and well-paid professions, women continue to be exceptions, constituting a mere 5 percent of the total number of professors, judges and senior civil servants. Only among doctors is this percentage significantly exceeded, women making up 20 percent of the total number of doctors (Bock-Rosenthal, Haase and Streck 1978).

As for pay: by international standards, women in West Germany are well off; their wages and salaries are among the highest in Europe. This does not mean, however, that everywhere in West Germany there is equal pay for equal work. Women manual workers and academics in private industry, in particular, are often paid less for the same work as that done by male colleagues with equal qualifications. Admittedly, such discrimination is difficult to prove in specific cases, because the work done by men and women can seldom be directly compared. Detailed investigations of wage disparities are not yet available, but one theory which does seem to be justified is that the relatively high pay of West German women is due more to the general industrial efficiency of West Germany than due to a wage policy favorable to women.

The difficulty in establishing the equivalence or non-equivalence of men and women's work, and in thus establishing the existence of unjustified disparities in pay, is partly the result of the segregation of the sexes in employment. Most women are employed in factories and offices where only women, or mainly women, are employed. In France, Italy, West Germany and the Benelux countries, only between a fifth and a third of working women are employed in factories and offices with equal proportions of men and women workers. The majority of women employees work alongside other women. They have male superiors and bosses, but very few or no men among their fellow workers (Pross 1973). What effects this separation of the sexes has, what differences there are, for instance, in the working climates of factories employing exclusively female or exclusively male labor, and those with a mixed work force has, to my knowledge not yet been investigated. What is evident is that pay in the women's ghettoes is lower, the chances of promotion less, and the impulses to take up further training weaker.

The incomplete and imperfect integration of women in employment is not confined to West Germany. None of the industrial nations offer their female populations the same career opportunities they offer their male populations. This general similarity, however, is accompanied by considerable differences between nations in the extent to which equal rights and opportunities have been realized. The Soviet Union and Sweden seem to be relatively far advanced as compared to West Germany; Italy is particularly backward; the Netherlands is also quite backward; while Great Britain and France are on a par with West Germany. The factors determining the degree of sexual equality achieved in employment would have to be the subject of a separate investigation, but the most crucial factors are probably the supply of labor, the dominant ideology, and ultimately the level of the national average income. Where, as in the Soviet Union, there is a concurrence of an egalitarian ideology, a short supply of workers, a low average level of income and a large surplus of women, the result is a comparatively high degree of equality between the sexes in employment. Where, on the other hand, there is concurrence of a conservative ideology concerning the sexes, and a long-term surplus of labor, the result is, as in Italy, a low degree of integration of women with men in employment. The relative importance of the various determinants--ideology, supply of labor, average income level, and surplus of women--is not yet clear. In sum, in a ranking of the Western European industrial nations, it would be fair to postulate that West Germany would occupy a position in the lower half. The integration of women in employment in West Germany is neither as far advanced as in the Soviet Union and Sweden, nor as backward as in Italy or the Netherlands (Held and Levy 1974; Step by Step 1979; Haavio-Mannila and Sokolowska 1978; LaDonna Oggi in Italia 1973; Pross 1973).

Although women have not yet achieved real equality in employment, there have been important ideological developments. First, it is now accepted as perfectly natural for women of all social classes and age groups to go to work. It is no longer looked upon as the last resort for the destitute and the poor, as it was a few decades ago. Second, there has been a sharp rise in the average level of education and training for younger women, fostering their greater interest in careers. Finally, there has been a general improvement in working conditions for both men and women: shorter working hours, better physical conditions, and a more "civilized" atmosphere at places of work. These and other processes have led to a thoroughgoing change: women are increasingly attracted to careers. For many middle-class women, a trained professional role is nowadays just as attractive if not more attractive than the traditional female roles of housewife and mother. This shift in attitude is a new development, a significant stage in the lengthy transformation of women's views of themselves.

Women in the Family: Housewives

During this transition, the role of women in the family has not been left unaffected; their position within marriage has become stronger compared to twenty years ago. Now joint affairs are often also jointly decided upon, although as a rule the husband retains the telling influence. Nor does the tendency toward a more balanced power structure in marriage mean that the traditional distribution of work has become obsolete. Housework continues to be the wife's job not only in the West but also in the socialist industrial nations. The observation made in 1972 by the Soviet sociologists Chartschew and Golod is probably applicable to all industrial nations: "The sharing of housework by husband and wife takes place on a traditional basis: most of the work falls to the wife, with the husband playing a merely supporting role, the extent of this support varying from case to case" (Chartschew and Golod, 1972). The American sociologist Alice Cook has confirmed this in a survey of nine Western and Communist states (Cook, 1975), and an investigation in 1971 of six Western European countries came to the same conclusion (Pross, 1973).

Despite the traditional division of domestic work between the sexes, the role of the housewife and mother has changed as women themselves have become conscious of their problems. Seen in purely quantitative terms, the "housewife only" role is in retreat. In the industrialized socialist countries the role of the non-working housewife is tolerated only as an exception, and in Western societies it is retreating behind other roles and combinations of roles. Even more significant are the qualitative changes.

As various investigations in West Germany document, many women who devote themselves exclusively to their families are becoming increasingly aware of the disadvantages of their form of existence. It is constantly having to be at her husband's and children's disposal and having to sacrifice her own needs for theirs that such women find particularly trying. They feel that they have to give more than they get in return, that they help more than they are helped, that they are unselfish "servants" giving their "all" for the well-being of the family. They see themselves as figures of self-sacrifice who are expected to give up more than men or working women.[1] These views that women have of themselves, exaggerated as they may be in individual cases, nevertheless have very real foundation in fact. They are the result partly of the natural dependence of small children on the mother, partly of men's love of domestic convenience, and partly of changes in the outside world. This is a world today in which the principles applied are equal give and take, equal sharing of burdens, and "fair" compromise between diverging demands. In view of the universality of such egalitarian attitudes outside the home, it is difficult for women to acquiesce to the norm of self-sacrifice still expected of them in the home.

Another source of depression for housewives is the low value attached to their work in the home. Recent opinion polls have once again confirmed that most men in West Germany prefer home-loving women. The popular image of the ideal woman is still that of a motherly figure rather than that of the understanding, easy-to-get-along-with professional woman. Professional women are respected; motherly women are desired.[2] Yet this has not resulted in housewives' work being valued. There is hardly a man who considers housework to have the same objective value as the work he does in his job, and the vast majority of men believe that a man would not find housework "sufficiently demanding." Work in the home, including bringing up children, is regarded as useful and honorable, but is at the same time a second-class occupation.

Women who suffer from the one-sidedness of domestic life cannot normally count on the sympathy and understanding of their husbands; men on the whole refuse to understand why housewives are discontented if they have sufficient financial security and can divide up their time as they choose. Most men's enlightenment does not go far enough for them to recognize the justification for housewives' disgruntlement or to cooperate with their wives in seeking solutions and alternatives. Wives, thus, are left alone to overcome their problems by themselves.

But the most serious distress and unease, even though this is not always admitted by the women affected, derives today from the growing attractiveness of the role of the working women mentioned above. Career and family are now in competition with one another. The growing prestige of the career woman is diminishing the prestige of the housewife, and it is not uncommon for the former to look down upon the latter. Housewives can no longer identify so unquestioningly with their work, can no longer accept their role so much as a matter of course, because there are rival roles, perhaps inaccessible to them, but no less attractive for that reason.

It remains to be seen how the role of the housewife will develop further. The only certainty is that there can be no return to the former state of affairs. Quite apart from whether or not such a return would be desirable, the way is blocked by irreversible attainments: the rise in the average standard of young and middle-aged women's education and training, as mentioned; the greater interest shown by women in taking on a job; the declining willingness to acquiesce and to make life-long sacrifices; the growing conviction of women that they can cope with other responsibilities besides domestic ones; the disintegration of metaphysical exaggerations with regard to the housewife's role and the weakening of other kinds of excessive ideological elevation of the function of women in the family. In the face of these developments, any appeals to women to recall their allegedly primary functions, their true vocation, are condemned to failure.

On the other hand it is obvious that housewives with families fulfill tasks which will still have to be carried out some way or other in the future. No society can manage without housework, without the upbringing of children and young people, or without giving them the undivided loving care and attention they need. One possibility is for a society to transfer these responsibilities to collectives such as large communes, but this choice is not that of the vast majority who would view it as constituting a retrograde step and an intolerable loss of personal freedom, of privacy and culture. It is unlikely that the people of West Germany will opt either for making the hopeless attempt to restore former conditions or for doing away with life in private homes and small families altogether. If, then, they want neither of these alternatives, in the long term they are going to have to struggle to find new models for women's (and thus also men's) roles in the family. In order to achieve this, it is first necessary to calmly recognize and accept the present situation: namely, that most women, and particularly younger women, wish to have a family *and* a career. There is hardly a woman who wishes to forego having a family, and hardly a woman who wants to sacrifice having a career. The vast majority of women want to have both, just as the vast majority of men want to have both. A life-long concentration on home and family is rejected, particularly by well-qualified women and women with professional experience, as is likewise an exclusive life-long concentration on a career. There is, therefore, an urgent need to create better opportunities for combining both. This can be achieved in various ways: by means of part-time work while the children are still small; by guaranteeing that a woman who temporarily gives up her job will be able to take it up again after a number of years; by arranging for the children to be looked after by suitable persons or institutions so that the mother can continue her career; and by sharing family and career roles equally between husband and wife. At present there are few possibilities for women to combine career and family without strain. Here there is urgent need for measures to be taken to increase the possibilities of interchange between career and family life. In the long term this means that we must bid farewell to the familiar figure of the non-working housewife and that the non-working housewife, like many other women's roles and role models, has been a historical type, not the "eternal" phenomenon that many observers would hope for.

I have already mentioned that most men, including the younger ones, are not yet prepared to help their wives to solve their problems and thus to contribute towards relieving the tension between the sexes. In the eyes of the majority of men, the social relationship between the sexes is still essentially unproblematic: the husband is the stronger partner, who wants his job and wants to be the breadwinner; the wife is the weaker partner, who wants to play her present role in the family, who only occasionally wants to have a job, and then only an undemanding one, and who wants to be able to look up to her husband. According to this male view, the roles of the sexes are so well coordinated that they complement each other in a harmonious way. To question such an order is, in the view of most men, to stir up trouble maliciously. What they fail to see is that the "trouble" is rooted within the order itself and is not "stirred up" from outside. Their harmonic conception of the social relationship between the sexes fails to recognize the unfairness of women's burden.

Women in Politics

Much as the majority of men in West Germany cling to conservative conceptions of their own and of women's functions and abilities, it would nevertheless not be true to say that they are unhesitatingly confident in their judgments and behavior. This is demonstrated by examinations of the corresponding conditions in the field of politics. The German Bundestag has passed, during the past ten years, a variety of acts all aimed at securing for women not just equal rights theoretically but also equal rights in practice. That a Parliament consisting of over 90 percent men should be prepared to take such measures is evidence of a degree of acceptance of the justice in women's demands. This acceptance, however, does not go so far as to produce a significant demand for women to be given greater access to positions of political power. The number of female MP's (Members of Parliament) in the German Bundestag, in the state parliaments and on the local councils is still low. It fluctuates between 6 and 9 percent, a proportion already attained in the Weimar Republic more than half a century ago (Enquete-Kommission 1976). A development which was not the case in the Weimar Republic is that it has since become customary for at least one woman to be included in each federal or state government. The Federal High Court (Bundesverfassungsgericht), the executive committees of the political parties, the large trade unions and comparable organizations nowadays also usually have at least one female member. This constitutes progress, but not a breakthrough or fundamental change in the traditional pattern of power. Apart from certain exceptions, those women who do occupy senior positions in politics do not have any determining influence.

This situation in politics is not confined exclusively to West Germany. The conditions are similar in other countries of Western Europe, where West Germany occupies a position at the lower end of the middle range in this respect. Clearly superior to West Germany are Finland and Sweden with over 20 percent women MP's (Haavio-Mannila 1978). Austria, Denmark and Norway also have higher proportions of women in high political office than West Germany (Bundeskanzleramt, Vienna, 1975). Lower figures are reported from France, Great Britain (Home Office, London 1974), Belgium, Italy and the USA (Epstein 1976). Everywhere the representation of women in senior executive positions in politics, in governments, parties, and other organizations is similar, namely, modest.

A further interesting finding is that in no other European Economic Community (EEC) country do men's and women's views differ so widely on the question of the participation of women in politics as they do in West Germany. Here a narrow majority of men say that politics should continue to be left to men; that women should not play the same role in politics as men; that people have more confidence in a male MP than in a female. Women questioned on this point showed a more egalitarian reaction. Only a minority of about a third shared the opinions of the male majority. In West Germany, more women criticize the slow rate of the development towards equality than in other countries. Young women in particular (15-34 years) would like to see more rapid change. More women in West Germany than in other countries (except Ireland) think that women have less chance of success in life than men.[3] The exact significance of this is not clear. It *could* mean that the conditions in West Germany are particularly bad for women and, for this reason, trigger off sharper criticism. However, this explanation is in my view incorrect, because it is a fact that the situation in Italy and in the

Netherlands, and probably also in Belgium, is less favorable than in West Germany with respect, for instance, to pay, promotion possibilities, and employment. I tend rather to attribute the greater impatience among West German women to recent ideological developments, and in particular to the spirited and widespread public discussion on the roles of the sexes which here, too, has been going on for some years.[4] It is this discussion which has raised the vague expectations of equality without bringing about many noticeable changes in reality. There is now a wide gulf between expectations and reality.

This raises the question of whether, and if so to what extent, this discrepancy is mobilizing women to take the initiative themselves and to start campaigns for equality. The answer is: relatively little. The widespread criticism of male dominance has not led to new political alliances of women, nor has it as yet strengthened the position of women in existing political associations noticeably. Nothing has been founded in West Germany along the lines of the National Women's Political Caucus in the USA. Of course, there do exist a large number of women's associations, which are loosely affiliated to a national confederation, the German Women's Council (Deutscher Frauenrat). Its composition, however, is so heterogeneous that it can neither go on the offensive nor mobilize women for specific campaigns for the betterment of women.

This brief survey of the participation of women in politics has shown that in this respect West Germany ranks among the most conservative countries in Western Europe--more conservative than Sweden, Finland, Denmark and perhaps Great Britain; less conservative than Italy, Belgium, the Netherlands and Luxembourg. It is the industrial elite who are particularly backward, less so the political elite; in between are the trade union leaders and the cultural elite made up of teachers, writers, and scholars.

The reasons why so few women have real political and economic power are probably basically the same in West Germany as in other Western countries. Politics is traditionally a male domain. To breach this exclusiveness would require a great deal of effort on the part of both men and women, but neither have any inducement to make that effort. A more equal distribution of power would be against men's manifest interests, and women would have to put up with considerable sacrifices at present for the sake of an uncertain future--it would entail loss of their leisure time, money, family harmony and acceptance by the outside world. The pressure of suffering upon women is not great enough to activate them in large numbers to take militant action. Moreover, it should not be forgotten that, generally speaking, their position has improved: equal legal rights, extended opportunities in education and training, a wider selection of career opportunities, more favorable working conditions in industry, and last but not least an extremely far-reaching improvement of their status within marriage and the family. The objective facts of life simply do not motivate them to assault the bastions of tradition.

Moreover, women probably also lack the psychological prerequisite for such action. Girls and women continue to be brought up both within and outside the family according to older ideas of femininity. These ideas make it difficult for women to develop the characteristics necessary for a political or professional career--ambition, confidence in one's own strengths and abilities, ability to get one's own way, love of power, staying power in conflicts. In addition, girls and women are strongly oriented towards family tasks and functions. From early childhood onward they are prepared for activities in the private sphere, and more recently for career roles, but not for participation in public life. Their awe of this sort of activity still remains very deep-seated.

Of course, there are further obstacles to women's extending their activities into the field of politics, and these include forms of direct discrimination: opposition from the husband; relegation of women to marginal functions; open derision. Ultimately, what is probably the most influential factor is the fact that positions of power and qualified professional positions are among the most coveted of all. Competition is fierce. In order to hold their own here, women need a good deal of hardness, physical robustness, time, rhetorical aptitude, expert knowledge and tactical skill. Undoubtedly, such combinations are today still rarer in women than in men.

The explanations suggested for the low proportion of women in powerful positions in West Germany probably also apply to other Western countries. These factors undoubtedly exhibit specific national features and characteristic national colorings. The Western European nations may be growing increasingly similar, but underlying each is a different past which affects the present and extends into the relationship between the sexes. In West Germany, the relationship between the sexes is likely to continue to develop towards equality. The speed of this process, however, is unlikely to be rapid. There is certainly no immediate prospect for full equality.

Notes

1. In a comprehensive, and statistically representative survey on non-working mothers more than two-thirds of the women agreed to the statement: "As housewife and mother a woman is primarily her family's unpaid maid." Similar statements received a similar response (Pross 1975: 174). As was revealed in another study, a majority of non-working wives expressed the view that much as they try to help their families in all kinds of needs, they themselves get but little help from husbands and adolescent children (Richter 1973: 294).

2. As shown by a representative study of men between 18 and 50 years of age, almost all men want a woman to be motherly and home-loving. To be sure, she is also expected to be independent, but most men define such independence as the capability to manage home and family without bothering her husband with it. The independence desired is not independence by an income of her own or by being anchored in the world outside of the family but the independence, and ability, to get along with her family tasks (Pross 1978: 141).

3. When asked: "In your experience, do women of between 20 and 30 years of age have as much, more, or less opportunity than men of the same age to succeed in life?" 43 percent of the German women, and 49 percent of Irish women, said "Less." In all other countries of the European Economic Community, the percentage of pessimistic women was much lower (Commission of the European Communities 1975: 27).

4. On television, in newspapers, popular magazines, and innumerable conventions.

References Cited

Bock-Rosenthal, Christa Haase and Sylvia Streeck
1978 Wenn Frauen Karriere Machen. Frankfurt/ New York: Campus Verlag.

Bundeskanzleramt, Vienna.
1975 Bericht über die Situation der Frau in Österreich. Fraienbericht 1975. Wien: Österreichische Staatsdruckerei.

Chartschew, A.G. and S. I. Golod
1972 Berufstätige Frau und Familie. Edited by Wissenschaftlicher Beirat für Soziologische Forschung in der DDR. East Berlin: Dietz Verlag.

Commission of the European Communities, ed.
1975 European Men and Women. A Comparison of their Attitudes to Some of the Problems Facing Society. Brussels.

Cook, Alice H.
1975 The Working Mother. A Survey of Problems and Programs in Nine Countries. Ithaca, New York: Cornell University, Publications Division, New York School of Industrial and Labor Relations.

No author
1964 Die amerikanische Frau. Bericht der Sonderkommission von Präsident Kennedy, deutsche Übersetzung. Informationsdienst für die Frau. No. 7/8.

1976 Enquete-Kommission "Frau und Gesellschaft" des Deutschen Bundestages: Zwischenbericht. Deutscher Bundestag 7 Wahlperiode, Drucksache 7/ 5866 (quoted: "Interimreport 1976").

Epstein, Cynthia Fuchs
1976 Sex Roles. *In* Contemporary Social Problems. R. K. Merton and R. Nisbet, eds. New York: Harcourt Brace Jovanovich.

Haavio-Mannila, Elina
1978 How Women Become Political Actors. Helsinki: University of Helsinki, Department of Sociology, Working Papers No. 6.

Haavio-Mannila, Elina and Magdalena Sokolowska
1978 Social Position of Women. *In* Social Structure and Change in Finland and Poland. Erik Allardt and Wlodzimierz Wesolowski, eds. Warsaw: Polish Scientific Publishers.

Held, Thomas and Rene Levy
1974 Die Stellung der Frau in Familie und Gesellschaft. Eine Soziologische Analyse am Beispiel der Schweiz. Frauenfeld/ Stuttgart: Verlag Huber.

Hemldonck, Marijke van
1976 Women in Decision-Making Elites--Women in Industrial Relations. Draft Discussion Paper. Conference on Women in Decision-Making Elites in Cross-National Perspective. Cambridge.

Home Office, London
1974 Equality for Women. Presented to Parliament by the Secretary of State for the Home Department by Command of her Majesty. London: Her Majesty's Stationery Office.

No author
1976 Institut für Arbeitsmarkt- und Berufsforschung der Bundesanstalt für Arbeit: Frauen und Arbeitsmarkt. Ausgewählte Aspekte der Frauenerwerbstätigkeit. Quintessenzen aus der Arbeitsmarkt- und Berufsforschung 4/ (quoted "QuintAB 4/1976").

Kommission der Europäischen Gemeinschaften
1980 Die Frauen und die Europäische Gemeinschaft. Vergleich zwischen den Mitgliedstaaten. Aktionen der Gemeinschaft. Brussels.

La Donna Oggi in Italia
1973 Inchiesta nazionale sui problem della condizione femminile e sul ruolo della donna nella nostra societa. Inchiesta Shell No. 10. Genoa.

Lapidus, Gail Warshofsky
1979 Women in Soviet Society. Equality, Development, and Social Change. Berkeley/ Los Angeles/ London: University of California Press.

Pross, Helge

1973 Gleichberechtigung im Beruf? Eine Untersuchung mit 7000 Arbeitnehmerinnen in der EWG. Frankfurt: Athenaeum Verlag.

1975 Die Wirklichkeit der Hausfrau. Die erste repräsentative Untersuchung über nicht-erwerbstätige Ehefrauen. Reinbek: Rowohlt Verlag.

1978 Die Männer. Eine repräsentative Untersuchung über die Selbstbilder von Männern und ihre Bilder von der Frau. Reinbek: Rowoht Verlag.

Richter, Horst Eberhard

1973 Konflikte und Krankheiten der Frau. *In* Familiensoziologie. Ein Reader als Einführung. Dieter Claessens and Petra Millhoffer, eds. Frankfurt: Athenaeum-Fischer Taschenbuch Verlag.

No author

1980 Step by Step. National Plan of Action for Equality, drawn up by the National Committee on Equality between Men and Women. Gotab/ Kungälv.

Sweden's National Policy of Equality Between Men and Women*

Anne-Marie Qvarfort, Joan M. McCrae, and Pauline Kolenda

Among modern industrial nations, Sweden may well be the one closest to treating women as the equals of men. The Danish economist Bent Rold Andersen (1984: 111) speaks of the Nordic "passion for equality," equality "in economic circumstances, in dignity, and in respect . . .," an attitude "present long before the welfare state began." Swedish egalitarianism is expressed in efforts since World War II to narrow the income gap between rich and poor, and in legislation to ensure and bring about sexual equality. Berit Rollen of Sweden's National Labor Market Board, head of the division dealing with equality between men and women in 1978, commented:

> Publicly, all political leaders [in Sweden] support the idea of equality of the sexes. It is written into the programs of all the political parties and unions. Everyone in the establishment knows very well what one is "supposed" to say and think about equality between the sexes. No politician would dare to say that women are better suited to take care of children than men. Nobody would dare state what a Republican county chairman said in Houston to the effect that participants in the Women's Conference were "a gaggle of outcasts, misfits and rejects" (Rollén 1978: 3).

This paper is an attempt to assess the status of women in Sweden. Especially impressive is the considerable recent legislation, governmental structure and programs meant to move the Swedes towards equality of the sexes. These are reviewed in the first part of the paper. In the second part, the question is raised: What accounts for this action on behalf of equality for women? and in the third part, the question is asked: Are there inadequacies in the Swedish program?

I. Progressive Legislation for Sexual Equality

In the Swedish monarchic parliamentary democracy, there is a special secretariat in the Ministry of Labor concerned with sexual equality. The Labor Minister sees to it that the issue is never overlooked in government policy-making. A Council on Equality Issues brings government, political parties, employers, and the women's organizations into dialogue. A special commission carries on research and investigation into issues of equality (FSS 1984). In its National Plan of Action for Equality, published in 1979, the cabinet-level National Committee on Equality between Men and Women stated Sweden's policy as follows:

> Everyone has the right to work and earn his or her own livelihood; hence women and men must have the right to work on equal terms. It is necessary to bring about an altered male role which includes the same rights to and responsibility for home and children as the female role does . . . It must be possible for women as well as men to combine work with family life on equal terms . . . (National Committee on Equality 1979: 161).

Sweden thus became the first country to formulate as government policy the effort to change both men's and women's roles in order to bring about equality between the sexes.

The Act for Equality between Women and Men at Work was passed by the Swedish parliament, the Riksdag, in 1980 to promote equal rights at work, in working conditions, and in opportunities for growth and advancement. Employers are required to make plans to promote equality at work, and the Equal Opportunities Commission can fine employers who fail to take positive measures. A government Ombudsman is responsible for monitoring compliance with the act; he or she first tries to persuade employers accused of sexual discrimination through offering information, advice, and negotiation before turning disputes over to the Labor Court (FSS 1984).

Schools have been alerted to the need to abolish sex-role stereotypes. A sexually equal curriculum was introduced in schools in 1970-71 (Scott 1982: 8). The Swedish Institute states:

> The comprehensive school gives both boys and girls obligatory instruction in domestic science and child care. At the lower levels both learn textile handicrafts, woodworking and metalwork. The school's officers for educational and vocational guidance are to challenge conventional stereotypes. (FSS 1984)

Swedish women already work for pay outside their homes in large numbers, at possibly the highest rate in the modern world. While in 1930 about one-third of women aged 15 to 64 were gainfully employed, by 1965 more than half were, and by the late 1970s three-fifths were; by 1984, 78 percent of women were in the labor force, compared to 86 percent of men. The increase for married women has been even more striking. While in 1930 less than 10 percent of married women worked, by 1947 47.2 percent were working outside the home at least half time, and in 1983 the proportion had reached 80 percent. The rise in the proportions of women with young children who work has increased even more. While in 1965 27 percent of women with children under the age of seven were gainfully employed at least half-time, by 1983 the proportion had reached 82 percent (McCrea 1977: 388; FSS Swedish Labor Market Policy 1979: 2; FSS 1984; FSS Equality 1979: 2; National Labor Market Board 1984: 11; FSS Child Care 1980: 2).

Skard and Haavio-Mannila comment:

> . . . recent female recruits into the labor force are predominantly middle-aged married women, often with dependent children. Marriage (and child care) and gainful employment may have been mutually exclusive occupations earlier in this century, but clearly they are no longer. (Skard and Haavio-Mannila 1984: 151)

Siv Gustafsson of the Institute for Economic and Social Research in Stockholm compared the figures for working Swedish women with those for American women. He wrote:

> In 1975, 68 percent of Swedish women aged 16-65 were in the labor force compared to 53 percent in the USA. This differential widens even further after the child-bearing years when 75 percent of Swedish women aged 35-54 participated compared with 56 percent of US women. However, 45 percent of Swedish women were employed part-time compared to 34 percent in the US. The same year 88 percent of Swedish men aged 16-64 were labor force participants whereas the US figure was 78 percent. (Gustafsson 1979: 1)

Swedish women's wages have not been as high as men's. In 1982 the average income for women was 48,100 Swedish *kronor* (about $8000),[1] or 64 percent of the average man's income of 75,300 Swedish *kronor* (about $12,000). Almost half of women earned less than 40,000 Swedish *kronor* (about $7000), while only one-quarter of men earned less than 40,000; on the other hand, four times as many men (40 percent) as women (10 percent) earned over 80,000 Swedish *kronor* (about $13,000). To some extent, at least, women's lower wages are due to an occupational segregation of the sexes. In 1980, 60 percent of women were in five occupational categories--nursing, clerical work, shop assistants, domestic work, and teaching. Presumably, as more women enter "male" occupations for which salaries are higher, their wages will increase. Not only government but unions also favor equal pay for women and men (Statistics Sweden 1985: 43, 39; McCrea 1977: 390).

Sweden has one of the highest standards of living in the world. In the 1980s it vies with Norway for highest rank among all nations in *per capita* income. In most families the male breadwinner's salary is supplemented by his wife's, as well as by various welfare benefits. The work week in Sweden is about 40 hours, and there is a statutory five week paid vacation. Such attractive conditions are countered by the high taxation necessary to maintain the prenatal-to-senility welfare program which will be discussed below (FSS Swedish Economy 1979: 1; FSS General Facts 1980: 2).

Not only do large proportions of women work, but there is very little unemployment in Sweden. Between 1940 and 1986, unemployment was never above 3 percent; in 1980-82 when Swedish unemployment was 2.6 percent, unemployment in the United States was 8.1 percent. Since

1970, unemployment has been higher among women than among men, but of recent years the differential has declined. Such low unemployment has been accompanied by expansion in jobs; during the 1970s, 200,000 new jobs were developed. The government counteracts unemployment tendencies by training programs for workers to upgrade their skills or learn new skills that industry needs; most of the trainees in such programs are women. To break down the sex-linking of certain occupations, the government subsidizes programs to train women for men's occupations, and supports efforts to attract men into women's traditional jobs such as nursing; it makes loans to those new business ventures agreeing to hire at least 40 percent of each sex. In 1983 all occupations within the armed forces were opened to women. (FSS General Facts 1980: 1; Qvarfort 1986; Rehn 1984: 148; FSS Swedish Labor Market Policy 1979: 2; McCrea 1977: 384, 378; FSS 1984).

Although women tend to cluster in a few occupational categories, they are well represented in the professions; about half of those in law, medicine, dentistry and social services are women. Forty-five percent of the law students are women, as are 43 percent of the medical students. Similarly, about half of the students in higher education are women; in 1983, 56 percent of all first-year students at Swedish universities and colleges were women. Still most university degrees are taken by men, and women tend to confine themselves to a narrow range of major subjects. The proportions of women professors are lower than in the United States; for full professors, the proportion who are women is 3 percent in Sweden as compared to 11 percent in the United States; for assistant professors, the comparison is 7 percent as compared to 19 percent (McCrea 1979: 314; FSS 1984; Scott 1982: 153; Skard and Haavio-Mannila 1984: 151).

Women are represented in government in Sweden, however, in larger proportions than in the United States. In 1985, 29 percent of the members of the Riksdag (the Swedish parliament) were women, 101 out of 349 members. The first woman was appointed to the prime minister's cabinet in 1947. During the latter part of the 1970s and the first part of the 1980s, there have been five women out of twenty in the Cabinet; among them was Karin Söder, a former teacher, who was the foreign minister; in 1986, the Minister of Labor is a woman, Anna-Greta Leijon; among her responsibilities is the policy on sexual equality (Statistics Sweden 1985: 57; Qvarfort 1986;

Eduards 1980: 2; McCrea 1979: 323; Childs 1980: 71; Skard and Haavio-Mannila 1980: 155).

Women have had the vote since 1921 in Sweden, and they vote in elections in proportions equal to or greater than men. Representation of women in popularly elected assemblies at the regional and local level runs around 30 percent, although there are a few in which almost half the representatives are women (Statistics Sweden 1985: 56, 60-63; Eduards 1980: 1; Skard and Haavio-Mannila 1984: 155).

Turning from the world of work to the family, it may be noted that Sweden has the highest rate in the world for cohabitation between the unmarried of opposite sexes. Although cohabitation without marriage was a traditional custom in some parts of Sweden in bygone times,[2] more recently there was disapproval of it until the late 1960s. By the early 1970s, Swedes had accepted it and the numbers of weddings taking place dropped by half between 1966 and 1973. In 1971, only 57 percent of all Swedish women aged 15 to 44 were married, as compared to 68 percent in England and Wales. In the age group 20-24, most couples living together are unmarried, and about one-third of children are born to unmarried mothers. About half of the unmarried couples who have children together, however, eventually marry. For many benefits, the Swedish welfare programs do not distinguish whether a couple living together are married or not (Scott 1982: 65-70; National Committee on Equality 1979: 72; Trost 1980).

As for women's right to abortion, Sweden has had laws permitting abortion under certain circumstances since 1938--"Abortions were permitted for medical, socio-medical, humanitarian and eugenic reasons or upon injury to the foetus." A commission to look into abortion was appointed in 1965. Its report made in 1971 entitled "The Right to Abortion" was used as the basis for formulating a new law commencing in 1975. A government information circular states the following:

> The new Abortion Act went into force on January 1, 1975 . . . The main principle contained in the new Abortion Act is that the woman herself decides if an abortion is to be carried out. The act specifies as follows:
> --Abortion is free upon request up to the end of the eighteenth week of pregnancy.
> --Before the twelfth week, the woman need consult only a doctor. Thereafter, she is required to discuss the matter with a social

> worker as well. The woman may be refused an abortion only if the operation involves a risk to her life or health.
>
> --An abortion before the end of the eighteenth week may not be refused without reviewal by the National Board of Health and Welfare.
>
> --After the end of the eighteenth week of pregnancy, the approval of the Board of Health and Welfare is necessary to obtain an abortion, and there must be special reasons for the permission. Such approval may not be granted if the foetus is judged to be viable. . .
>
> Only a qualified medical practitioner may perform an abortion, and the operation must take place at a hospital or other medical institution approved by the Board of Health and Welfare (FSS Legislation on Family Planning 1980: 1).

Sweden has had compulsory sex education since 1956. Both the fertility rates and abortion rates for teenagers have markedly decreased in Sweden since 1976, and they have been much lower than in the United States; this is true even if one compares only white teenagers (Trost 1985: 45).

Sweden's population in 1984 was 8.3 million with a sex ratio of 1,024 women to 1,000 men. The birth rate in Sweden is low with a rate in 1984 of 11 (actually 10.96) per 1000 population. Sweden also has a high life expectancy, 80 years for women and 74 years for men in 1983. The death rate is very low--10.96 per thousand. The growth rate of the Swedish population might appear to be at a zero-population growth level, but Sweden has enjoyed an immigration of workers from the other nordic countries, Germany, Turkey, and Yugoslavia since the 1960s, and these increase the annual growth rate of the population to slightly more than 2 per thousand per year in the early 1980s (Statistics Sweden 1985: 7, 9; FSS The Swedish Population: 1).

In 1981, the Overseas Development Council ranked Sweden as having the highest 'quality of life' in the world, based on three factors: infant mortality, life expectancy at age one, and literacy. While Sweden got 97 marks out of 100, and Guinea-Bissau got 12 as the lowest nation, the U.S. ranked ninth with a score of 94, behind not only

Sweden, but also Denmark, Iceland, Japan, the Netherlands, Norway, Canada, and Switzerland (*San Francisco Chronicle* 1981).

With an increasingly aged population and a low birth rate, there are few large households in Sweden. About one-third of households are one person; another one-third are two persons; somewhat less than one-fifth are three persons; the rest are composed of four or more. In 1981, out of 1.1 million families with children under the age of 18 living at home, 44 percent had only one child, 42 percent had two, and 14 percent had three or more (FSS 1979 Equality: 1; FSS 1984).

Part of the Swedish welfare system has been child allowances, introduced in 1948. By 1986, these amounted to 4800 Swedish *kronor* or about $909 per year for a child up to the age of sixteen. A higher amount is given for the third child in a family, so that if one has three children, one gets 16,800 *kronor*, the payment for the third child (7200 *kronor*) being one and a half times that (4800) of the first and second child (Qvarfort 1986). Larger families are also aided by government housing allowances for the expenses of living in their own home or for subsidies for rent (Melsted 1979: 3).

Expectant mothers receive free prenatal care, services of a midwife, hospitalization, and medication. Child care is subsidized in various ways including the parenthood insurance scheme introduced in 1974 (Scott 1982: 8). This aid to parents is explained as follows:

> The parenthood insurance scheme . . . can be seen as an encouragement toward parental sharing of responsibility for children. During the first twelve months after a child is born, the father or the mother has the right to parenthood leave of absence with pay (90 percent of one's income for the first nine months and at a fixed rate for the remaining three). (FSS 1984)

The father or the mother of a newborn child has the right by law to have a leave of absence from work with pay for twelve months. One portion of the leave must be shared by both parents, but one parent can relinquish the remainder of her or his share to be used by the other. Both father and mother may return to full-time work at any time.

> Up to six months may be saved and used at any time up until the child's eighth year. In addition, gainfully employed parents have the right each year to up to 60 days off with pay per child for care of sick children. As of 1979, a law gives parents of children under the age of eight the right to cut their workday back by two hours--from eight hours to six hours a day--but without financial compensation. (FSS 1984)

The system of progressive taxation and government subsidies means that the financial losses for a family with reduced work hours are relatively small.

In addition to these supports for new parents, the Riksdag passed a bill in the spring of 1979 supporting voluntary parental training to take place during their regular paid working hours with no loss in pay. Melsted explained:

> Fathers of newborn babies will be invited to the hospital maternity ward for a day to become acquainted with the baby and learn to take care of it. At ten to twelve meetings before childbirth and the same number afterwards, parents will meet under expert guidance to discuss the problems and pleasures of parenthood (Melsted 1979: 5).

In fact, the majority--eight out of ten--Swedish mothers do return to work within twelve months after a child is born (FSS Child Care Programs 2). A study reported by Gustafsson is summarized in the table on page 170. These figures show that over five years there was a decline in the proportions of women deciding to stay home full-time with a newborn, as well as a slight increase in those choosing to return to work full-time.

Parents have a right to day-care facilities for children, paid largely--89 percent of it--by the government; however, the number of places in municipal day-care centers is far below the demand for them. Even though the Riksdag passed a Preschool Activities Act in 1973, it was estimated in 1977 that there were only 168,200 places for 400,000 children under seven years old. There was a similar need for after-school "leisure centers." The issue of day-care centers, along with that of nuclear reactors, figured prominently in the election campaign of 1976. In

1984 the need still persisted (Gustafsson 1979: 4; Scott 1982: 104, 106; McCrea 1977: 382; Skard and Haavio-Mannila 1984: 154).

Women's Orientation to the Labor Force Subsequent to Birth of a Child

	1970-72	1975-77
Left the labor force	29%	13%
Changed from full-time to part-time	11%	21%
Returned to full-time work	60%	66%
	100%	100%

Formulated from Gustafsson 1979:3.

There are a variety of welfare programs in Sweden for children such as free meals at school, free dental care up to the age of sixteen, and free education. In 1986, those sixteen to twenty years old who were studying received a grant of 400 *kronor* a month ($64). University students received a study grant of 240 *kronor* a month ($38), loans of up to 3450 *kronor* ($549) per month and special child allowances (Qvarfort 1986; McCrea 1977: 386).

Sweden's prenatal-to-senility welfare program includes other features such as pensions entitling a recipient to as much as 60 percent of average income earned during her or his 15 best paid years, sickness benefits of as much as 90 percent of wages or salary and covering both hospital costs and non-institutional care, medicine costing more than 35 *kronor* ($4), and 50 percent of the costs of dental care (for those over sixteen). There are programs for the handicapped and life and job injury insurance for everyone (FSS Swedish Economy 1979: 2).

One other aspect of women's family life is that of divorce. By 1976, half of Swedish marriages ended in divorce, and 22 percent of families with children were single-parent families. By the Family Law of 1974, divorce is legally easy and quick if a couple has no children under the age of 16; if there are children, the couple must take a six months' deliberation period. Since July 1, 1983, joint custody of the children is automatic unless either or both members of a couple request a different arrangement. Both parents must contribute child support, but the government ensures that a child has a minimum subsistence if sufficient child support is not provided by parents. The arrangement for child custody is the same if a cohabiting couple with children decide to separate. With both married and unmarried couples, upon divorce or separation, the joint dwelling will be assigned to the needier of a pair, according to recent law (Scott 1982: 70, 8, 66, 60; FSS 1984).

In the first part of this paper, a generally favorable summary of the situation of women in Sweden taken from a demographic and legislative point of view has been presented. In the next section, the question is asked: what accounts for the high status of women in Sweden? In the last section, the question is asked: what are the inadequacies in this program for equality of the sexes in Sweden?

II. What Accounts for the High Status of Women in Sweden?

Sweden was not a strong feudal state during the Middle Ages due to its low population and poor soil; cultivation with concentrations of serfs did not suit Swedish agricultural and demographic conditions. It was rather a nation of small Lutheran farmers who from early times were used to self-government. Although Sweden was a leading manufacturer of iron in the mid-eighteenth century, producing about 40 percent of the world's iron, it was primarily an agricultural country up to the mid-nineteenth century when the economy became deeply disturbed by mechanization of farming, limited need for labor in industry, poor harvests, and famines. In response, there was a mass emigration of Swedes; about 20 percent went to other nordic countries; 80 percent went to the United States. Between 1865 and 1930 nearly 1.4 million people emigrated; around 360,000 returned to Sweden. In the century from 1870 to 1970, however, Sweden was transformed from a largely agrarian country to one in which less than 5 percent of the population was engaged in agriculture (McCrea 1977: 403; FSS The Swedish Population: 1; FSS General Facts 1980: 1).

The industrial revolution in the latter part of the nineteenth century stimulated the establishment of the Social Democratic Party in Sweden, the political party that was to organize its national government for more than half of the twentieth century. Advocacy of sexual equality has been part of that party's platform. What is the background of this egalitarian ideology instituted as national policy when the Social Democrats were in office?

The Social Democratic Party was founded in 1889 by Karl Hjalmar Branting who in his youth was strongly influenced by Karl Kautsky. Marquis Childs explains that Kautsky was:

> the leading Marxist theoretician of the German Social Democratic party before World War I. A friend of Friedrich Engels in London, he became after Engels' death in 1895 the principal Marxist theoretician. His thinking was colored by the Social Darwinism of the time, which led him to the conviction that, while the Social Democratic party was revolutionary, it stood for a revolution that was inevitable through a process of evolution. Thus it obviated the need for any violent overthrow, since socialism was certain to come with the passage of time. Needless to say, this "revisionist" Marxism was anathema to Lenin and the Bolsheviks (Childs 1980: 8).
>
> In his founding speech in 1889, Branting, then aged 28, said: "Sweden's Social Democratic Party in its efforts to organize the Swedish working class for its conquest of political power will make use of such means as correspond to the people's natural sense of justice. The contemporary program which we have formalized and for which we are working is best proof that we, for our part, are by no means striving for a violent revolution" (Childs 1980: 10).

Committed to socialist evolution rather than revolution, the members of the Social Democratic Party were at first university students, mostly of middle-class background. Branting was first elected to the Riksdag in 1896. Through an alliance with the Liberal Party, Branting formed the first Social Democratic Party government in 1920. During the period after the First World War, the party members who were attracted by the formation of the Soviet Union in Russia left the Social Democratic Party and formed Sweden's Communist Party. Branting, however, remained a man of the middle. He set the example for Sweden's foreign policy by working to establish the League of Nations after World War I; for his efforts, he was awarded the Nobel Peace Prize in 1921 (Childs 1980: 9-10).

Sweden was neutral during the First World War, and after the war it prospered by supplying Europe with iron, wood, and other products for postwar rebuilding. By then, peaceful working relations had been established between the labor unions and the organization of employers. Sweden had already gone through its struggle for the establishment of unions beginning in the 1880s and culminating in a general strike in 1909 (Childs 1980: 7).

The shape of Sweden's future prosperity was set in the 1920s. The Danish Social Democratic politician, Erling Olsen, tracing the history of the Social Democratic parties in Scandinavia, writes:

> Union membership grew because the unions were able to obtain remarkable increases in real wages owing to the new waves of industrialization and the rapid increases in productivity. At the outbreak of World War I, union membership was widespread in all the Scandinavian countries. (Olsen 1984: 174)

Even with the introduction of an eight-hour day, productivity increased, showing that human welfare and productivity could both be pursued compatibly.

An important doctrinal difference between the Social Democratic Party in Sweden and Marxism was the former's rejection of a "theory of immiseration." Olsen (1984: 174) explains that the Social Democrats saw the increase in real wages that the union gained in the 1920s as "a verification of the Marxian theory of the inevitable growth of the labor class," but it was not consistent with the Marxist idea that the wages of the working class would continuously decline because of the built-in exploitativeness of capitalism and the labor-saving propensities of new techniques--the Marxist theory of immiseration. Olsen comments, "This (the increase in real wages) told them that technical progress would not impoverish labor but enrich it." Swedish labor's acceptance of technical progress has probably been a crucial feature in the industrial advancement of Sweden during the twentieth century.

Through cooperation between industry and government in the 1920s, the timber and wood industries were fostered, and the merchant fleet enlarged. Industry developed a high-grade steel that became an important export. Having become a modern industrial nation, Sweden's prosperity already depended upon its exporting quality goods, although it was not so dependent upon exports as other Scandinavian countries. The innovativeness of the Swedes was also demonstrated in the beauty of their new arts and crafts--beautiful Orrefors glass, modern pewter designs, the sculpture of Carl Milles--and in shipbuilding (Childs 1980: 11-13). By the 1920s, productivity based upon the export of high quality manufactured goods, the profits from which could support social welfare, was already set as Sweden's hallmark for the future.

As in most other parts of the world, Sweden suffered high unemployment during the Great Depression of the late 1920s and 1930s. However, the proportion of women in the labor force outside of agriculture remained stable during the Depression (Skard and Haavio-Mannila 1984: 147). In 1932, the Social Democrats were elected to national office, a position the party was to hold for 44 years, until 1976. Then after an interlude of six years of conservative (a center-right coalition) government, the Social Democrats were again elected to form the national government in September 1982, and they remain in office in 1987.

The party's theorist during the Depression, Ernst Wigforss, accepted Keynesian economics and was influenced by the Swedish economist Gunnar Myrdal. Through a coalition with the agrarian political party, a policy of mutual support resulted in the farmers' supporting a Keynesian program for the cities--state employment for the jobless--while the Social Democrats supported loans and other measures to aid in the revival of agriculture. Various welfare benefits were legislated, including unemployment insurance, old age pensions, health insurance, and housing (Childs 1980: 17-18). The government declared a policy of full employment which included employment for women (Qvarfort 1981: 2). Sweden not only came through the Depression successfully, but managed to remain neutral once more during the Second World War.

The Social Democrats work closely with organizations of labor unions. Olsen (1984: 172) mentions the facts that, "When the Swedish Social Democratic Labor Party was established in 1889, most labor unions collectively enrolled their members into it. . . . And when the Swedish National Organization of Labor Unions (*Landorganisationen*--LO) was established in 1898, membership in the Party was made compulsory for all union members."

There are three such mass organizations in Sweden: the Swedish Confederation of Trade Unions composed of 1.7 million members of 25 blue-collar unions (L.O.); the Central Organization of Salaried Employees, composed of about 70 percent of the white-collar workers who belong to 23 unions (called T.C.O.); and the Confederation of Professional Associations, composed of the 100,000 people belonging to the professional organizations of lawyers, doctors, and dentists (called S.A.C.O./S.R.). Although the Social Democrats have close ties with L.O., the government does not interfere in labor negotiations concerning agreements on wages and working conditions that take place every one to three years between the unions and the Swedish Employers' Confederation (S.A.F.). The S.A.F. includes most private employers. Although Sweden has had an elaborate welfare system supported by heavy taxation, it is not very socialistic in terms of ownership of productive plants. Over 90 percent of Swedish business is privately owned (FSS General Facts: 2).

Much of Sweden's prosperity has rested upon peaceful and harmonious relations between business and unions.[3] Childs explains that these go back to the Saltsjobaden Pact of 1938 (named for a suburb of Stockholm) between the business organization and the unions. The principle of this agreement was that as long as industry prospered, taxation on industry could and would support increasing welfare measures. At the same time, taxation would not be so high on industry as to discourage reinvestment. Another factor in labor peace has been the Labor Courts before which either business unions or individuals could get impartial judgments on grievances. A further factor has been the small but successful cooperative movement in Sweden. Cooperatives manufacture light bulbs, automobile tires, cash registers and calculating machines, run department and self-service food stores. The cooperatives have close relations with labor unions and share similar philosophies (Childs 1980: 19-22).

From the end of World War II up to the oil crisis of 1973, the Swedish economy was productive and prosperous. At the end of the Second World War, the Swedish industrial plant was unharmed by war, since Sweden had again remained neutral. It could supply Europe with steel, wood products, and other manufactured goods needed for reconstruction after the war. Germany has been one of

Sweden's chief markets for its exports. Sweden developed the production of two motor cars and several airplanes including a supersonic jet (FSS Swedish Economy 1979: 1; Childs 1980: 14).

The coalition between private business and a reformist socialist government was made possible in large part by this prosperity. There were sufficient profits and earnings both to develop industry further and to support an expensive welfare state. People could both pay high taxes and have a very high standard of living.

Sweden, by way of the Social Democratic Party, committed itself to the principle that government should cure social ills (Rehn 1984: 166); many party members "favored the use of legislative machinery and the powers of the state as a means of improving the living conditions of the working class" (Olsen 1984: 174). Economic prosperity and expansion with a growing need for labor attracted women into the labor force. Facilitating movement from home to labor market were demographic factors like the decline in marriage and fertility rates and the rise in divorce, as well as the higher costs of living and need for more families to have two paychecks (Skard and Haavio-Mannila 1984: 151).

What were the causes of Sweden's prosperous economy? First, obviously certain natural resources such as iron ore and timber. Secondly, an educated population also characterized by ingenuity, innovativeness, even genius in design, and efficiency in performance. Thirdly--this is a characteristic which Marquis Childs emphasizes--a capacity for organization. It is this capacity that also helps to account for the success of the welfare program in Sweden. Childs writes:

> Both in industry and in government, from the highest level down to the county councils, citizens without number have given themselves to the tasks of organization. The innumerable commissions that have preceded every important reform have meant days, weeks, and months of serious and concentrated effort. Few countries can show a comparable record of solid endeavor often leading the way to compromise and general acceptance of a measure that may have seemed at the outset too radical and innovative. Royal commissions have paved the way for almost every welfare step adopted

> into law. Often such studies required years before they were ready to be presented to the Riksdag and the public. (Childs 1980: 5)

Other important Swedish characteristics relevant to their welfarism have been a belief in reason. Childs defines Sweden's "middle way" as "a conviction that reason can prevail in righting the wrongs of a troubled world" (Childs 1980: 42). Following the tone originally set by Branting is a Swedish intolerance of injustice, and a drive to repair injustices. One may add community concern and public-spiritedness, and the "passion for equality" Andersen (1984: 111) emphasizes. Andersen (1984: 118) also speaks of the "extremely relaxed attitude of the people toward their central government and public authorities . . . at the heart of the Nordic welfare state." Committed both to social justice and to private capitalistic enterprise which inevitably brings about inequalities of income and living standards, the Swedes have tried to repair the inequalities through the redistribution of wealth by means of welfare programs (Andersen 1984: 119).

Possibly important also both to prosperity and to successful government was the cultural homogeneity of the Swedish people up to the 1960s when fairly sizeable numbers of immigrants began to come in to work; a homogeneous people presumably have fewer problems in communication and fewer tests to their commitment to tolerance.

An aspect of the cultural homogeneity of the Swedish people is their belonging (95 percent of the population) to a single church, the Church of Sweden, a Lutheran faith. This institution does not seem to be a center for opinion of a conservative anti-socialist sort. We are told:

> In 1958, after a sharp controversy within the established Church, it was decided to let women take Holy Orders, and the first were ordained in 1960. (FSS Religion 1980: 2)

None of the literature suggests the presence in Sweden of organizations of either a religious or non-religious sort that are against welfarism or against equality for women as it has come to be defined in Sweden.[4] In trying to understand the high status for women in Sweden, we might possibly add: the absence of vocal organizations *against* equality for women in the economic and political spheres of society. This is not to say that there are not forces *for* traditional sex roles; these will be discussed in the last section of the paper.

The high status of women in Sweden is part of the egalitarian socialistic philosophy of the government which has been dominated for over fifty years by the Social Democratic Party, one believing in the transformation of society through legislation and welfare measures. This government has had the cooperation of labor unions and of business so that there has been a trisectoral national economic advance.

The unanimity of all of Sweden's five political parties in the policy for equality of men and women is not surprising if viewed as part of the ideology of equality initiated by Branting and his followers earlier in the twentieth century, but it does seem extraordinary when viewed against earlier Swedish social history. Qvarfort points out that under a law of 1734 a woman, whether married or not, must be under the protection of a guardian--her father, brother or husband. This was changed in 1872 for unmarried women, who came of age at 25; and in 1921 for married women, who came of age at 21 (Qvarfort 1981: 1). McCrea pointed out that the Freedom of Commerce Act of 1858 gave women the right to work if their husbands permitted. The 1920 Marriage Code permitted a married woman to own her own property and work as she pleased (McCrea 1981: 1).

Skard and Haavio-Mannila (1984: 142-150), who assert that Sweden and the other four Nordic countries (Denmark, Norway, Finland and Iceland) have been patriarchal for "at least a millennium" (1984: 142), divide the history of women's emancipation in Sweden into three stages. The first comes with nineteenth century industrialization; before it, Sweden's was primarily an agricultural economy. Women were subordinate to husband or father. "Women were, in effect, minors; as such, they could neither enter into legally binding contracts, such as marriage, nor make use of their property and income" (1984: 143). Balancing this role of obedient follower of a male household head was the total responsibility which women took for the farm when men were away at sea, trading, or working in the forests. Industrialization separated the production of goods from the home, and it was men, now the "breadwinners," who left home to be the producers, while women by the turn of the century were increasingly left in the isolated home to do housework and care for children, to be "housewives." Some women began to take poorly paid factory jobs under difficult working conditions. Both married and unmarried women often worked as maids in wealthier homes. With the development of the typewriter, telephone, and telegraph, unmarried women were the inexpensive labor that ran these new machines; the more educated among them worked as teachers or midwives.

The first stage in the demands for women's emancipation were made by middle-class wealthier women who portrayed the emotional and intellectual oppression of women in their writings and urged respect for women and equal rights with men. While their feminist ideas were resisted, they, nevertheless, spread and prepared the second stage, the establishment of feminist organizations during the last part of the nineteenth century. These worked for political rights and access to higher education for women. Some of these organizations were affiliated with male political parties. Some working women established women's unions, demanding better working conditions, shorter working hours and equal pay. Prominent in the middle decades of the twentieth century were the Fredrika Bremer Association and the Swedish Women's Left Federation, the one rather conservative, the other working for peace and women's issues.

> By the end of the second stage of the feminist movement, before the outbreak of the Second World War, formal emancipation was essentially achieved. First unmarried women, then the married, became legally independent, and husband and wife were given formal equality in economic matters in marriage. Young women were permitted to enter high schools and universities, universal suffrage was introduced, and except for the ministry, women were permitted to enter the professions (Skard and Haavio-Mannila 1984: 146)

The third stage in women's emancipation in Sweden was part of a general women's liberation movement taking place in the European and American industrial nations, beginning in the 1960s. Nordic social scientists argued that "if women were to exploit fully the formal rights they had obtained, female and male roles would have to be altered" (Haavio-Mannila 1984: 148).

Hilda Scott finds the beginning of the contemporary movement for equal rights for Swedish women in a 1961 essay by Eva Moberg, the editor of the Fredrika Bremer Association's journal, entitled "The Conditional Emancipation of Women." Moberg rejected the idea that because women gave birth to children, they should be their sole caretakers. She wrote, "We ought to stop harping on the concept of 'women's two roles.' Both men and women have *one* principal role, that of being people." A group of Swedish and Norwegian women social scientists followed Moberg's essay soon after, arguing that adult men and women had one role that involved both employment outside the home and childcare and 'housework' within the home. Women's organizations and women journalists took up the issues, and the Social Democratic Party's women's organization brought home to the party as a whole that it must make sex-role equality part of its general program (Scott 1982: 5-6).

In 1964 a study group within the Social Democratic Party produced "The Erlander Report" (named for the prime minister, Tage Erlander); it proposed the aims for sex-role equality that were later embodied in legislation and policy. These were included in the party's program on equality in 1969, drawn up by Alva Myrdal. Scott writes:

> The document said in so many words that government powers over industry were to be used to eliminate sex discrimination, that labor-market and educational policies must counteract sex-determined choices of occupation, and that expanded services, especially day care and public transport, were essential requirements for an effective equality policy. "In the society of the future," it added, "when current practical barriers to equality have been gradually eliminated, the point of departure must be that every adult is responsible for his/her own support. Benefits previously inherent in married status should be eliminated . . ." (Scott 1982: 6).

This party policy on sexual equality was part of a general equality program concerned with several underprivileged groups, the old, the young, the handicapped, the unemployed, as well as women, and was concerned with their needs for higher income, access to more jobs, training and housing.

In part two of this paper, the career of the Social Democratic Party, founded during nineteenth century industrialization in Sweden, has been briefly traced, as well as the stages in Swedish women's emancipation during the later part of the nineteenth century and the first four-fifths of the twentieth century. It was during Social Democratic national governance in the early 1960s that the women's organization of Social Democrats was able to initiate government legislation that led to governmental structures concerned with equality for women.

III. Are There Inadequacies in the Swedish Program for Equality of the Sexes?

Two factors in the Swedish situation for women that could undermine sexual equality are the dependence for survival of equality programs on the nation's economic prosperity, and the persistence and reinforcement of a traditional ideology of a sexual division of labor. Facets of these will be discussed briefly in this part of the paper.

The programs to encourage women to take non-traditional jobs do not grow entirely out of the principle of equality of the sexes, Joan McCrea has argued, but are incidental to the labor shortage involved in rapid economic growth in Sweden along with a low birth rate. McCrea cited a survey published in 1970 by the Economic Planning Council in the Ministry of Finance emphasizing the labor shortage and recommending that strong measures would have to be taken to increase the employment of women (see also Liljeström 1978). Essentially, adult Swedish women are a source of labor alternative to young men who are in short supply because of the low birth rate, and to immigrant labor.

During the 1960s, Sweden depended upon the immigration of nordic, German and southern European workers. Since World War II, there has been a net immigration of 600,000 people, mostly young men seeking work (FSS General Facts 1980). About half of the immigrants are Finns; 7 percent are Danes; 6 percent are Norwegians, 5 percent are Germans, 10 percent are Yugoslavs; the other 22 percent are a mixed group of other nationalities (McCrea 1977: 386). About 7 percent of the total population are immigrants. McCrea suggested that the native Swedes' attitudes toward the immigrant workers is ambivalent. They are paid the same wages and receive the same social benefits as the Swedish workers, and they are entitled to six weeks of paid time to learn the Swedish language. They have the right to vote after three years' residence even without citizenship. There have been measures taken to make it possible for children to be instructed in their parents' native languages. However, many of the immigrants have looked upon their sojourn in Sweden as temporary; they have not been eager to acculturate to Swedish ways, and furthermore, they send out of the country a fair amount of their earnings (McCrea 1977: 387). Given the crisis in the Swedish economy that came with the increase in oil prices in 1973 along with competition from Japanese automobiles and ships, and an increasingly unfavorable balance of trade due to the higher cost of importing oil and the declining market for Swedish goods overseas, Swedish women workers who spend their earnings in Sweden for Swedish goods may seem preferable as workers to those who make Sweden's balance of trade even worse by sending much of their earnings out of the country to their relatives overseas.

McCrea pointed out further that the special training programs for women to learn "male occupations" have been devoted to the worst-off women, such as the middle-aged housewife entering the labor force, usually women with rather little education. The policy that "the worst-off women, the poorest paid, the least educated, and the least influential, should be aided first" was one of the principles of the National Council on Equality between Men and Women (McCrea 1977: 393). McCrea suggested that retraining of women for male occupations takes place in Sweden when a company is suffering a labor shortage, when Swedish men are not available to fill the jobs that are open, and there is a preference for Swedish women over foreign workers (McCrea 1977: 397-98). Such conditions may occur especially in the northern parts of Sweden where there is a shortage of male natives, because of a differential population movement south; there has been a tendency for Swedes to move to the urban areas, located in the southern part of the country. An example of such a labor-short situation is in the iron mines of very far northern Sweden. McCrea wrote:

> The labor market in Kiruna has been characterized by a shortage of labor in "men's occupations," accompanied by high unemployment of women. These circumstances made it practical for the government to launch a campaign to get women into men's jobs, even apart from the separate goal of

> equality of the sexes. A parallel in United States or British labor history would be "Rosie the Riveter" of World War II. Women are invited to work at non-traditional occupations when men are not available to fill the vacancies. . . . They are recruited for ore-processing or truck-driving, as well as for underground mining. . . . The fear is that if women don't find jobs in Kiruna, they will emigrate south, which contradicts the national goal to develop the northlands (McCrea 1977: 404).

McCrea pointed out that the recruitment for programs of retraining of women for men's jobs is not open. She commented:

> . . . if a woman already has a job as a nurse's aide, or a child-care assistant, or a typist, she is not eligible for free training in another occupation which pays better. Labor market training then can improve the status of only the worst-off women. The entry into men's occupations can occur only when a woman is unemployed and there are no trained men already available for the job. It is a step up for some women, but it is far from equality. The general shortage of labor in Sweden, rather than the goal of equality, is responsible for labor market training. The only instances in which an employed person can get free training for a better job is "bottleneck training" for sectors which are particularly short of skilled labor: shipbuilding, pulp and paper, child care, nursing, health services, and road transport (McCrea 1977: 400).

McCrea's observation of the special programs for training women for men's occupations is that the programs are carefully tailored to fit the needs of industry and to fit the requirements of other government policies such as development of the northern region of Sweden. It seems clear that a forceful policy of equality for women has coincided with a prosperous economy and a shortage of labor--in the 1960s and 1970s.

The economic situation of Sweden in the early 1980s paralleled that of the United States. The rate of economic growth had slowed, as had exports; obsolete industrial plants such as those in shipbuilding and steel-manufacturing could not produce commodities at prices competitive with those made in other nations; with this semi-stagnation had come a heavy governmental budget deficit or public debt. In 1983, 30 percent of the Swedish national budget was financed by loans; thus, much of future budgets must be payment of interest on these loans. The gradual increase in costs for the many Swedish welfare programs had resulted in taxes of 50 percent of income for the average citizen and had taken 29 percent of the nation's gross domestic product (as compared to 18 percent for welfare programs in the United States) (Kuttner 1983: 14; Andersen 1984: 115, 125, 127, 134; Olsen 1984: 189). A big question for Sweden has been: Can it continue to finance its costly welfare system? Even more specifically, can Sweden continue to pay the costs of child-care programs, parental leave programs, and so on, that are so important for women who work outside the home?

Ingenious as always, the Swedes came up with some unusual solutions to their economic crisis. In 1982, LO, the Swedish trade union federation close to the Social Democratic Party, developed a program whereby workers voluntarily limit their wages in return for part-ownership in the companies where they work. The wage-earners' funds of stock serve as investment for the expansion and improvement of manufacturing companies. By such a plan, workers receive raises in wages in the form of stocks, but business also receives needed investment funds. The wage restraint also reduces consumption of imported and domestic goods, and both improve Sweden's balance of trade and retard inflation (Rehn 1984: 167).

The new LO program was met with protest from business and many of the citizenry in 1983 (Arne 1984: 57), but the Social Democratic economic program beginning with the party's return to government in 1982 supported it. Their economic program also included devaluation of the currency and reduction of taxes for those in the highest income brackets, and by 1986 analysts deemed it to be quite successful. Sweden's industrial production has increased faster than that of the rest of Europe; the Swedish budget deficit has been cut considerably; its steel industry has been modernized and its shipbuilding industry terminated (Kelman 1986: 7-8); and a new aircraft project has spurred the development of new technology and new production. Sweden has been restructuring its industrial plant successfully. Meanwhile, the Swedish Labor Board continues its activities of creating new jobs and seeing to it that displaced workers from obsolescent industries are retrained. By such programs, Swedish unemployment is less than half of that of other European countries (Kuttner 1983), and remains under 3 percent (Kelman 1986: 7). Possibly by such innovative programs the Swedish economy may be able to continue to support the many welfare programs for its citizens, including those especially for children, women, and families.

Since many of the welfare programs are programs either designed to help women or include women as their beneficiaries, whether Sweden can continue to pay their costs is important for the status of women. Aside from the issue of cost of programs already in place, there are questions about the gulf between the government-labor policy of sexual equality and the Swedish social norms supporting a traditional sexual division of labor.

How are we to understand the reluctance of Swedish women to enter occupations that have not traditionally been women's realms despite the fact that already by the 1950s and 1960s textbooks in the schools were being criticized for their sexist content, that the schools have been enlisted in a program to change traditional sex roles (Oster 1977: 5-6), and there are guidance counselors to encourage the choice of studies and occupations without the usual sex stereotypes (McCrea 1979: 320)?

The persistence of traditional sex roles may be explained as a survival from an agrarian past, but they are reinforced daily by the various communications media in Sweden. *Step by Step* refers to the "one-sexed world picture" which the news media give. Ladies' magazines idealize traditional womanhood. Advertising shows some caution about sex stereotyping, sometimes solving the problem by merely showing the product itself, but in juvenile books, "the most popular authors are still those who give expression to a traditional sex-role pattern" (National Committee on Equality 1979: 147-148). A study of television, done in 1977, described as follows:

> All programs for children, teenagers and families broadcast in the space of a few weeks during 1977 were systematically examined from the sex-role aspect. One-third of the programs presented women and men in real roles: thus of the program *comperes* (hosts) 12 were women and 35 were men, the

> reporters numbered 11 women and 36 men, the studio guests 47 women and 77 men, and the artists 41 women and 116 men. In creative programs (fiction) most of the leading parts were played by men who were shown working in occupations traditionally identified with the male sex. This pattern reappeared in animated programs for children. (National Committee for Equality 1979: 148)

The persistence of sexually-stereotyped occupational roles is not just limited to the realm of entertainment. In the specification of credentials for jobs, employers' images of male occupants are reflected. The responsibility for coordinating the new equality programs rests with the Division for Personnel Affairs of the Ministry of the Budget. On the basis of many studies done, the Division has identified two obstacles to the advancement of women into better jobs. One is the content of job descriptions; the other is the credentials required for jobs. Often an applicant for a job must have a university degree when the work itself could be done by a person with less education, and fewer women have university degrees than do men. Experience in the military may give an applicant (male) an extra edge in being awarded a job, while decades of child rearing and the ability to type (almost always female capabilities) are given no credit. Many government agencies have been enlisted in the effort to re-examine and rewrite job descriptions, and several have launched experimental programs to put women and men in unconventional (usually done by the opposite sex) jobs (Scott 1982: 37-38).

Another problem that stems from adherence to traditional ideas of sex roles is the unexpected reluctance of Swedish men to replace a sexual division of labor in Sweden for a principle of interchangeability of roles (Scott 1982: 154). While public opinion in Sweden is favorable to rights for women, the issue which confronts Swedish men is whether they can accept a change in their male roles. The reasonableness of the principle that men should contribute more to the home and women should contribute more to production outside the home seems simple until its effects on the central economic power structure is contemplated. Then it is discovered that men have strong interests in keeping that power structure mono-sexual. Even its effects on the lessening "comforts of home" that may be available to men may be vigorously resisted. In the usual Swedish way, the Labor Market Board of the national government (see Working Party for the Role of the Male 1986) has had a committee thinking through the issues: what is the male role? what are male problems? how can the male role be changed (presumably to make for greater equality between the sexes)? After careful study and discussion, the Working Party is likely to develop some reasonable recommendations.

Related to the reluctance of men to do housework and care for children and the consequent continuation in most Swedish families of women's double burden (doing both housework and work for wages outside the home), many women prefer a work week of less than forty hours, especially during the years when they have younger children. Since the better jobs are usually ones requiring forty hours or even more per week, this is another obstacle to their advancement to better jobs. Scott comments:

> The fact that the average number of hours worked by all women has dropped from 33 in 1970 to 31 in 1978 can be understood as a vote for the 30-hour week. The demand for the six-hour day was first put forward by the national organization of Social Democratic women in 1972. Since then it has become widely recognized as an essential condition for a fairer division of responsibility in the home. Its achievement depends, however, on the willingness of the trade unions to fight for it . . . (Scott 1982: 39-40).

The trade unions are favorable to the six-hour day as a long-term goal, Scott says, but their priorities are elsewhere.

The most intransigent adherents to traditional concepts of sex roles, it might appear, are men in higher positions in Swedish businesses and unions. While there are substantial numbers of women in government in Sweden, as we saw in the first section of this paper, there are few women in the higher ranks of either businesses or labor unions. How can more women arrive in decision-making posts in these sectors of the economy? So far, even the rational Swedes, reputed for their sensitivity to injustice, have not developed an effective program to achieve this.

Scott sees the future for women's equality in Sweden as presently in the hands of employers and trade unions, with the government legislation and agencies acting as catalysts for change. Moves toward women's liberalization have been ample. Some men feel they have already done a great deal for women in the recent past. Whether those in the highest positions can be influenced to unlock the gateways to "the top" remains to be seen.

IV. Conclusion

Swedish women have been eager to take up wage-- and salary--work outside the home. Rita Liljeström has commented:

> The eagerness of women to work is indexed by these facts: . . . the mothers of children under seven have come out into the labor market *before* working hours for the parents secure parents' and children's needs for each other, *before* the municipalities have expanded their facilities for child care, *before* the attitudes in the job world have adapted themselves to the labor force's responsibility for children, and *before* legislation has built in safeguards to protect the interests of parents and children. Besides, it is not at all unusual for wives to take over partial economic responsibility for the family *before* the husband begins to share in the practical and emotional responsibility for the children. (Liljeström 1978: 7)

While the Swedish welfare programs benefiting women and supporting the equality of the sexes is impressive, Liljeström voices a Swedish view that these programs have not yet gone far enough. The next logical steps for the development of sexual equality in Sweden are at least partly clear. Whether those steps will be taken in the face of conservatism with respect to the sexual division of labor and some unwillingness of males in the most powerful positions in the economy to relinquish any of their power remains to be seen. The ingenuity of the Swedes, however, is likely to rise to the challenge.

Notes

*Editor's note: During the Symposium on the Anthropology of Women at the University of Houston on February 16, 1981, Anne-Marie Qvarfort read a paper, "Women in Swedish Society," and Joan M. McCrea read a paper, "Equality of the Sexes: Sweden and China." This paper combines Qvarfort's and McCrea's papers with background information on the social structure of Sweden provided by various Swedish government agencies, and by Childs (1980), Scott (1982), Skard and Haavio-Mannila (1984), and others; Qvarfort also provided for inclusion information on Swedish women in 1986. Unfortunately, our co-author, Dr. McCrea, died, after a bout with cancer, in 1984. This book is dedicated to her.

Notes

1. In calculating the exchange between Swedish *kronor* and US dollars, the exchange rate of January 1987 was used--that is, 6.28 *kronor* to the dollar.

2. Scott (1982: 69) writes, ". . . in sparsely settled northern Sweden, where land was plentiful and society relatively egalitarian, premarital sexual relations were an institutionalized form of courtship. There was nothing casual about such a relationship; it was regarded as a binding commitment. Yet it was not unusual for the actual wedding ceremony to take place after one or more children had been born. Loose relationships, on the other hand, were strongly condemned by the community and a resulting illegitimate child was a disgrace; many such mothers never found a husband."

3. Gösta Rehn (1984: 160) disagrees with Childs' interpretation that "harmonious cooperation between organizations of workers, employers and consumers, and a government-directed, unorthodox economic policy, had brought about great progress, both on the economic and social fronts." He counters: "Swedish economists instead love to point out that their country's economic success owed less to its well-advertised expansionist policy ('Keynesianism before Keynes') than to Sweden's having been involuntarily thrown off the gold standard in 1931, then accidentally establishing an undervalued currency and being helped greatly by expansionist policies in their export market."

   Since this paper is not a work in economics, but an attempt to assess the situation for women in Sweden, and the policies for equality of the sexes have been sponsored largely by the Social Democratic Party, we will not get into the issue of that party's contribution to the economic prosperity of Sweden. The reader may at least be aware that social scientists have different views on the reasons for Sweden's recent decades of prosperity.

4. Of recent years, organizations demanding lower taxes have developed in Denmark and Norway, but not in Sweden (see Olsen 1984: 187).

References Cited

Andersen, Bent Rold
1984 Rationality and Irrationality of the Nordic Welfare State. Daedalus (Winter, The Nordic Enigma) 113(1), 109-139.

Arne, Ruth
1984 The Second New Nation. Daedalus (Spring, Nordic Voices) 113(2), 53-96.

Childs, Marquis W.
1980 Sweden: The Middle Way on Trial. New Haven and London: Yale University Press.

Eduards, Maud
1980 The Swedish Woman in Political Life. New York: Swedish Information Service.

Fact Sheets on Sweden (FSS)
1980 Child Care Programs in Sweden.
1984 Equality Between Women and Men in Sweden.
1979 Equality Between Women and Men in Sweden.
1980 General Facts on Sweden.
1980 Legislation on Family Planning.
1980 Religion in Today's Sweden.
1979 The Swedish Economy.
1985 The Swedish Ombudsman.
1980 The Swedish Population.
1979 Swedish Labor Market Policy.
Stockholm: The Swedish Institute.

Gustafsson, Siv
1979 Women and Work in Sweden. New York: Swedish Information Service.

Jam Ö
1984 The Act Concerning Equality Between Women and Men at Work (The Equal Opportunities Act). Stockholm: Jam O.

Kelman, Steven
1986 The Palme Legacy: Swedish Socialism Revised. The New Leader 69 (June 16-30): 6-8.

Kuttner, Bob
1983 Trials of Two Welfare States. Atlantic Monthly (November 1983) 252 (5), 14-22.

Liljeström, Rita
1978 Integration of Family Policy and Labor Market Policy in Sweden. New York: Swedish Information Service.

McCrea, Joan M.
1977 Swedish Labor Market Policy for Women. Labor and Society 2: 377-406.
1979 Equality of the Sexes in Sweden under a New Government. Labor and Society 3: 309-324.
1981 Equality of the Sexes: Sweden and China. Paper read at the Symposium on the Anthropology of Women, February 16, 1981, at the University of Houston.

Melsted, Lillemor
1979 Swedish Family Policy. New York: Swedish Information Service.

National Committee on Equality Between Men and Women
1979 Step by Step: National Plan for Equality. Stockholm: National Committee on Equality Between Men and Women.

National Labor Market Board *(Arbetsmarknadsstyrelsen)*
1984 Equality in the Labor Market. Solna, Sweden: The National Labor Market Board.

Olsen, Erling
1984 The Dilemma of the Social-Democratic Labor Parties. Daedalus (Spring, Nordic Voices) 113(2), 169-194.

Oster, Rose-Marie G.
1977 Human Liberation--Swedish Society in Transition. New York: Swedish Information Service.

Qvarfort, Anne-Marie
1981 Women in Swedish Society. Manuscript.
1986 Personal Communication.

Rehn, Gösta
1984 The Wages of Success. Daedalus (Spring, Nordic Voices) 113(2), 137-67.

Rollén, Berit
1978 Gently Towards Equality. New York: Swedish Information Service.

San Francisco Chronicle
1981 Sweden Tops in 'Quality of Life.' November 12, 1981.

Scott, Hilda
1982 Sweden's "Right to be Human" Sex-Role Equality: the Goal and the Reality. Armonk, New York: M. E. Sharpe.

Skard, Torild and Elina Haavio-Mannila
1984 Equality Between the Sexes--Myth or Reality in Norden? Daedalus (Winter, The Nordic Enigma) 113 (1), 141-167.

Statistics Sweden
1985 Women and Men in Sweden: Facts and Figures. Stockholm: Statistics Sweden.

Trost, Jan
1980 Unmarried Cohabitation in Sweden. New York: Swedish Information Service.
1985 Swedish Solutions. Society 118 (November-December): 44-48.

Working Party for the Role of the Male, Ministry of Labor, Sweden
1986 The Changing Role of the Male. Tiden/ Arbetsmarknadsdepartementet. Stockholm: David Knight.

AUTHORS OF CONTRIBUTED PAPERS

Judith K. Brown teaches anthropology at Oakland University in Rochester, Michigan. She received her undergraduate training at Cornell University and has a Masters and a Doctorate from the Harvard Graduate School of Education. She also holds a Certificate in Child Development from the University of London and has been a post-doctoral fellow at the Bunting Institute of Radcliffe College. Her research interests have included the cross-cultural study of initiation rites for girls, women's subsistence activities, and the post-childbearing years. She recently edited with Virginia Kerns, *In Her Prime: A New View of Middle-Aged Women* (Bergin and Garvey, South Hadley, Massachusetts, 1985).

Robbie Davis-Floyd is an anthropologist engaged in cross-cultural and historical research on pregnancy and childbirth. She received her Ph.D. in Anthropology and Folklore from the University of Texas at Austin in May 1986. A frequent speaker at national and international conferences on childbirth, Dr. Davis-Floyd is currently in the process of transforming her dissertation, *Birth as an American Rite of Passage,* into a book (University of California Press, forthcoming 1987). She is married to Robert N. Floyd, architect and energy consultant, and is the mother of two children, a daughter born in 1979 by Cesarean section, and a son born in 1984, at home. She teaches at Trinity University, San Antonio, Texas.

Nancy Edwards currently does evaluation research as a member of the Houston Independent School District Research Department. She is ABD in anthropology from the University of California at Berkeley and did 13 months of field research with the Muslim Samal of the southern Philippines in 1971-72.

Pauline Kolenda is Professor of Anthropology at the University of Houston. She holds a B.A. from

Wellesley College and a Ph.D. from Cornell University. Her anthropological fieldwork is done in India, and she has published articles and books on caste, family structure, religion and women in India. Recently published is her *Regional Differences in Family Structure in India* (Jaipur, India: Rawat Publishers).

Joan M. McCrea was Professor of Economics at the University of Texas at Arlington from 1963 to 1984. She also taught at Hollins College (Virginia) and at the University of California at Riverside. She held a B.A. in French from Indiana University. After completion of her undergraduate work, she worked as metallurgical observer in a steel mill, secretary, civil service examiner, and organization-and-methods analyst for the U.S. Air Force. She then returned to college to take a Ph.D. in economics at the University of California - Los Angeles. She is author of *Texas Labor Laws* and articles in the *Encyclopedia Britannica* and many professional journals. She visited Sweden in 1976 and 1978 under a fellowship grant from Sweden to study programs to train women for non-traditional occupations.

Helge Pross was Professor of Sociology at the Universität Gesamthochschule Siegen, Federal Republic of Germany. She was Visiting Professor of Sociology at the University of Houston - University Park in 1980-81.

Anne-Marie Qvarfort is a Principal Administrative Officer in the National Labor Market Board in Stockholm, Sweden. In her former positions, she worked on issues of women's labor.

Kathlyn Zahniser continued working for the telephone company for another two years. She then resigned to go back to school. She received her B.A. from the University of Houston-University Park in 1980.

Notices of Permission

pp. 9, 33, 41, 63, From *Birth in Four Cultures* by Brigitte Jordan, pp. 1, 35, 47, 50. Reprinted by permission of Eden Press Women's Publications, University of Toronto Press.

p. 10, From "Betwixt and Between; the Liminal Period in Rites de Passage" by Victor Turner, in the Proceedings of the 1964 Annual Meeting of the American Ethnological Society. Reprinted by permission of the American Anthropological Association.

pp. 15, 16, From *The Living and the Dead* by Lloyd Warner. Reprinted by permission of Yale University Press.

pp. 16, 17, From *The Rites of Passage* by Arnold van Gennep, translated by Monika B. Vizedom and Gabrielle L. Caffee. Reprinted by the permission of the publisher, University of Chicago. Copyright © 1960 by Monica B. Vizedom and Gabrielle L. Caffee.

p. 25, From "The Iatrogenesis of Damaged Mothers and Babies at Birth" by David Birnbaum in Stewart and Stewart, *Twenty-First Century Obstetrics Now!* pp. 105-106. Reprinted by permission of the author and the publisher, National Association of Parents and Professionals for Safe Alternatives in Childbirth.

p. 29, From "Hospital Obstetrics: Do the Benefits Outweigh the Risks?" by Dr. Frederic Ettner in Stewart and Stewart, *Twenty-First Century Obstetrics Now!* Reprinted by permission of the author and the publisher, National Association of Parents and Professionals for Safe Alternatives in Childbirth.

pp. 31, 63, 64, From *The Birth Primer: A Source Book of Traditional and Alternative Methods in Labor and Delivery* by Rebecca Rowe Parfitt, pp. 33, 96. Reprinted by the permission of the author and the publisher, Running Press.

pp. 34, 35, 36, Reprinted by permission of The Putnam Publishing Group from *Gentle Vengeance: An Account of the First Year at Harvard Medical School* by Charles LeBaron. Copyright © 1981 by Charles LeBaron.

p. 39, From "The Doctor-Nurse Game" by Dr. L.I. Stein, *Archives of General Psychiatry,* Volume 16, Number 6, p. 701, June 1967. Reprinted by permission of the American Medical Association. Copyright © 1967, American Medical Association.

p.43, From *Rites and Symbols of Initiation* by Mircea Eliade, pp. x-xi, Copyright © 1958. Used by permission of the publisher, Harper and Row, Publishers Inc.

pp. 43, 44, 45, From Dr. Michelle Harrison's "Birth as the First Experience of Motherhood" in Volume 2 of Stewart and Stewart, *Twenty-First Century Obstetrics Now!*, p. 585-587. Reprinted by permission of the author and the publisher, National Association of Parents and Professionals for Safe Alternatives in Childbirth.

pp. 22, 23, From Suzanne Arms' "Why Women Must be in Control of Childbirth and Feminine Health Services" in Stewart and Stewart, *Twenty-First Century Obstetrics Now!*, p. 64. Reprinted by permission of the author and the publisher, National Association of Parents and Professionals for Safe Alternatives in Childbirth.

pp. 27, 28, 55, From Suzanne Arms' "Immaculate Deception." pp. 79, 104. Reprinted by permission of the author and the publisher, National Association of Parents and Professionals for Safe Alternatives in Childbirth.

pp. 60, 62, From *Williams Obstetrics,* 16th Edition, edited by Jack Pritchard and Paul MacDonald, 1981, pp. 413, 666. Reprinted by permission from Pritchard and MacDonald: *Williams Obstetrics,* 16th Edition, Appleton-Century-Crofts, New York, 1980.

p. 61. Reprinted from *Malepractice: How Doctors Manipulate Women.* Copyright © 1981 by Robert Mendelsohn, M.D., with permission of Contemporary Books Inc., Chicago, p. 164.

p. 172, 176, 177, From *Sweden: The Middle Way on Trial* by Marquis W. Childs, pp. 5, 10. Reprinted by permission of Yale University Press. Copyright © 1980 by Yale University Press.

p. 183, Reprinted from Joan McCrea's paper, "Swedish Labour Market Policy for Women" published in *Labour and Society,* Volume 2(4) October 1977. Copyright © International Labour Organisation (International Institute of Labour Studies) Geneva, Switzerland. Reprinted by Permission.

p. 164, 179, 180, From Torild Skard and Elina Haavio-Mannila's *Equality Between the Sexes-Myth or Reality in Norden?* in the Nordic Enigma (Winter) p. 146. Reprinted by permission of the authors and the publisher, Daedalus.

cited throughout "Sweden's National Policy of Equality Between Men and Women." Quotations from Rollen's *Gently Towards Equality,* p. 3; Gustafsson's *Women and Work in Sweden,* --. 1, 3; Liljestrom's *Integration of Family Policy and Labor Market Policy in Sweden,* p. 7; *Step by Step* by the National Committee on Equality Between Men and Women, pp. 161, 147-148; Fact Sheets on Sweden including 1984 *Equality Between Women and Men in Sweden, 1980 Legislation of Family Planning,* p. 1; *1980 General Facts on Sweden,* p. 2; *1980 Religion in Today's Sweden,* p. 2. Permission for use of all of the above granted by the consulate of Sweden, New York City.